This is a unique book which reveals the real personality of a leader. The book answers many questions of life about leadership and success... helps you in becoming a leader in the chosen field of your life.

—Kamal Haasan, Actor/Director

A combination of wit and wisdom; drawing upon Chanakya, Machiavelli, Lao Tse and many others, Awdhesh Singh has produced an interesting and unusual book on leadership.

—Dr Karan Singh, Member of Parliament

His thought-provoking examination indeed removes mysteries associated with leadership and provides pragmatic tips for anyone to be a successful leader. The book, lucidly written, is a useful addition for those wanting to understand leadership behaviour and for those who want to be successful as a leader.

—TS Krishnamurthy, Former Chief Election Commissioner of India

The book is a treatise on leadership. The secrets of leadership are unravelled in a lucid and most engaging manner. The book engages readers with its anecdotal quality combined with highly insightful observations...I will strongly recommend this book to every potential leader to understand the 'art' of the matter and also to those who are already in leadership roles just to feel the 'heart' of the matter.

—Prof SG Deshmukh, Director, ABV-Indian Institute of Information Technology & Management, Gwalior

The author has made a bold attempt to present the hidden or the 'bitter' side of leadership, which complements the visible and 'sweeter' side. This book is recommended especially for aspiring leaders, while established leaders will be able to relate with the challenges and dilemmas they face in their day-to-day experiences.

—Anil Kapoor, Managing Director, Chambal Fertilizers and Chemicals Limited

This is a leadership book like no other...unlike other dry, unimaginative leadership books, this book is as fun to read as it is shrewd and practical. It is awash with countless insightful stories, quotes and examples. One of the outstanding features of this book is that it confronts with ideas that seem counter-intuitive, for example, the need for deception and to embrace one's vices. Yet, upon careful reflection we gradually recognise the accuracy of the author's subtle thoughts.

A well written and vitally useful book for all who aspire to be leaders, or for those of us who wish to understand how real leaders achieve extraordinary goals.

—Terry W Sprouse, award-winning author

This book is strewn with pearls of wisdom on the subject, painstakingly and meticulously gathered from all parts of the world. The book is a practical guide on how to blossom into a leader in any sphere of human endeavour and at any level, how to succeed as a leader and how to leave a legacy.

—MVN Rao, Former Chairman, Central Board of Excise & Customs

This book provides a beacon of a fresh view-point regarding the essence of leadership for all those who aspire to be leaders and those who want to change the world for the better. A book which must be read and evaluated, in the background experiences and insights of the serious reader.

—PR Ravikumar, Director General (Investigation), Income Tax, GOI

This book is indeed an insight on how to harness and hone one's skills in order to shape the qualities of a leader hidden in every person naturally. The author has achieved a straightforward and transparent way of approaching attainment of leadership, proving leadership is a science and not an art.

—S Madhukar, Former CMD, United Bank of India and Whole-time Member SEBI

It is a rare book which courageously explores the grey areas and dilemmas of leadership and allows the readers to make their choices without being prescriptive. Overall a great treat for all the students of leadership.

–E Balaji, President, People Services, TVS Logistics Ltd

Very insightful and refreshing. Theories of leadership have been explained in a fresh and unorthodox manner. The anecdotes have made the explanations highly revealing and easy to understand. A must-read for both practicing and aspiring leaders of men.

–S Kannan, Chairman, Chennai International Film Festival

This is a must-have book for any leader who wants to become more effective, strategic, operationally focused and balanced. It's a book for leaders who are striving to take control of their destiny and become the best they can be. Every professional should read this book to unleash the greatest leadership potential lying within.

–Sanjeev Kumar, Head & Vice President, Tata Projects Limited, Hyderabad

Yet another master piece from Awdhesh!

Very interesting reading with plenty of anecdotes relating to corporate world. To me it looked like a 'serious version of Dilbert's book on Management!'

–Aravind Santhanam, Director, Innovasphere Infotech, Former COO, Videocon Telecommunications Ltd

An excellent book to understand leaders and develop leadership qualities. The book is full of interesting anecdotes, jokes and stories which keep the readers glued to the book and help him remember the message with ease. The book truly reveals many secrets of leadership, which are hidden from the eyes of most of us.

–Prof Rajendra Sahu, ABV-Indian Institute of Information Technology & Management, Gwalior

THE SECRET RED BOOK OF
LEADERSHIP

A unique book which reveals the
real personality of a leader.
—*Kamal Haasan*

THE SECRET RED BOOK OF
LEADERSHIP

AWDHESH SINGH
Bestselling Author of
Practising Spiritual Intelligence

© Awdhesh Singh, 2015

First published 2015
Reprinted 2015

All rights reserved. No part of this book may be reproduced, stored in a retrieval system or transmitted in any form or by any means—electronic, mechanical, photocopying, recording or otherwise—without the prior permission of the author and the publisher.

ISBN 978-81-8328-386-1

Published by
Wisdom Tree
4779/23, Ansari Road
Darya Ganj, New Delhi-110 002
Ph.: 23247966/67/68
wisdomtreebooks@gmail.com

Printed in India

Contents

	Acknowledgements	xi
	Introduction	xiii
	Part I: The Need for Leadership	
1.	Who Can Be a Leader?	3
2.	Leader-Follower Dualism	12
3.	The Myths of Leadership	18
4.	Why Must You Aspire to Be a Leader?	27
5.	Transform into a Leader	31
	Part II: Dilemma of Leaders	
1.	Can an End Justify the Means	37
2.	The Connect between Good and Evil	44
3.	Balancing Love with Hatred	52
4.	Dealing with Both the Lower and the Higher Self	59
5.	Balancing the Masculine with the Feminine	66
6.	Equality or Differentiation?	71
	Part III: The Necessary Evils of Leaders	
1.	A Burning Desire to Lead and Achieve	79

2.	The Hunger for Power	85
3.	Creating Fear	90
4.	Divide and Rule for Success	95
5.	Why Leaders Need to Deceive	101
6.	Cover Your Evil	106

Part IV: The Facade of a Leader

1.	A Pleasant Personality	115
2.	Be an Actor	123
3.	The Propaganda War	130
4.	Leadership Branding	135
5.	Aura of Charisma	141

Part V: Developing Leadership

1.	A Powerful Idea	149
2.	Get a Grip on the Complete Reality	157
3.	Developing Imagination	163
4.	Taking Initiatives	170
5.	Developing Courage	176
6.	Team-building	183

Part VI: Practising Leadership

1.	Creating Trust	193
2.	Resisting Temptation	200
3.	Managing in Organisations	205
4.	Decision-making	214
5.	Cultivating Leaders	221
6.	Leaving a Legacy	226
	Bibliography	*231*

Acknowledgements

This book has evolved in my mind over many decades, perhaps since my early childhood. I always wondered why some people are respected and followed while others are not. Instead of deciding that a particular person is a leader, I focused on the traits which make a leader. Gradually, I started noticing that there are some qualities which make a person worthy of leading others. We all have a natural tendency to follow those whom we consider superior to us in intellect, knowledge, wisdom, courage or compassion as we all wish to improve financially, intellectually and spiritually by following better people.

I am indebted to a great number of people who have shown me the path of leadership. Perhaps the first leader, who influenced me since my childhood, was my great-grandfather Yadunath Singh. He was an epitome of principle, selflessness, courage and hard-work. I was also influenced by many teachers during my school and college days, who had magnetic personalities that attracted a class of students towards them. It has been my privilege to work with some great leaders in my own Department of Customs and Central Excise in India, from whom I have learned to follow as well as to lead. I would especially like to name a few senior officers like Sukumar Mukhopadhyay, PN Sarangi,

VK Garg, Jayant Misra, Anil Bhatanagar and Niraja Shah, whose contribution I can't forget.

This book would not have been possible without the constant help and support of Shobit Arya, the publisher and founder of Wisdom Tree. He encouraged me to write a book on leadership. We had countless discussions on leaders and leadership before and during the writing of the book. I would like to thank him for bearing my excessive enthusiasm and temperament for over a year in which this book was written and edited. I would like to thank each member of Wisdom Tree who has contributed to the improvement of this book. I am particularly grateful to Swapna Goel, who not only edited the book but also gave many valuable suggestions to improve the flow and content of the book.

Finally, I would like to thank my family. My lovely wife, Pratibha Singh, constantly supported me during my writing. My daughters, Akanksha and Ankita, have always been the loving inspiration for my writing. I am also grateful to my father-in-law Dinesh Singh, who has always motivated and supported me for writing this book and provided me with valuable guidance.

Introduction

Most of us wish to become leaders because they are highly valued by every society. Often, in deciding the destiny of others, leaders tend to make history. Leaders seem to have the best of everything we desire: Fame, wealth, and even power, which surely motivate most of us. We find them everywhere: In our history books, in the headlines of our daily newspaper, featured on television, commanding everyone's attention and envy all the time. No wonder we're all driven to try our hand at leadership, be it in business, management or politics.

There are thousands of biographies of great leaders, and millions of books on leadership. Even the man on the street knows quite a bit about the life of popular leaders. We then try to copy our leaders, believing we know them well. But we fail to become one.

Why?

That's because leaders are quite mysterious. They hide more than they reveal. Like an iceberg, there is much that lurks below the surface. And our dream to lead often sinks, same as the *Titanic*, as we do not get the full picture. In our quest to lead, we must therefore first understand the leaders for what they are, inside out.

Most books on leadership provide a limited view, discussing only aspects that leaders readily make available in the public domain. Hence, when we try to follow the incomplete signage in these books, we end up nowhere.

The Secret Red Book of Leadership lifts the veil on qualities that are not disclosed generally, but which often shape a successful leader. It is not a self-help book peddling a ready-made formula for success and leadership. The book describes the truth as it finds it—bitter or sweet. It explains reality without trying to be politically correct.

Leadership is a game that you must learn to win by using all means at your disposal. In leadership, winning is everything. It is not about principles, but only results. It matters not what a leader does, as long as he is effective. On the contrary, if you fail to achieve visible success, you are not accepted as a leader despite all your talents and commitment to the cause.

Much about how leaders conduct their lives is in public domain today, thanks to the media. Be they business or political heads, we are all aware that these torchbearers are often not good or virtuous people. In fact, many are perceived to be just the opposite. In the real world, leaders are rarely honest, patient, loving, compassionate or just, as they have been portrayed in books on leadership. Most do not shy away from bending rules to taste success. Yet, leaders are extraordinary people. That is why they have been accepted. But then, what is so unusual about them? Are they born with some exceptional gift of talent? Do they have a towering personality? Or have they done something unexpected and amazing in their life, which makes them extraordinary?

Take a quick glance at the lives of some great leaders, whether in politics, business or spirituality. You'll find that almost all great leaders had very humble beginnings. Mahatma Gandhi struggled to speak confidently in court; he had not enough cases to sustain his life. Bill Gates and Steve Jobs were both school dropouts. Abraham Lincoln was born in a log cabin in Hardin county, Kentucky, to humble parents, and his struggles in life are legendary. Yet, you'll see that they all did something in their lives, which helped them achieve greatness.

Abraham Lincoln once said, 'It has been my experience that folks who have no vices have very few virtues.' He was right, leaders are generally not flawless, rather they rise above their failings to emerge stronger as leaders. Yet, they hide their defects from public glare like the proverbial iceberg. It is a fact that evil is the source of all goodness and it is the vices that build the virtues of a leader.

If most people fail to become leaders, it may be because they run around shunning evil, and expend much time and energy avoiding vices rather than building on their inner goodness and virtues. Thus, the greatest challenge before all leaders is to draw from their vices, but publicly conceal them. It's okay to expose only their virtuous side. If their vices are out, they risk losing their leadership.

Leadership is therefore an art and not a science. It is not a reality that you can touch, feel and measure, but an illusion that is created with many tricks, which you should be able to learn and practise in a way that others are not able to grasp. Leadership is like magic. It looks great when you are able to conceal the tricks. But if the tricks get known, every magic turns quite ordinary.

There can also be no formula for leadership because human beings are not purely rational beings. Most people are selfish and emotional and expect their leaders to fulfil their desires by any means. So when you lead people, you must take care of all their needs, those that are expressed and those implied.

The Secret Red Book of Leadership provides the 360 degree view of leadership. We examine not only the strengths of the leaders, but also their weaknesses. To evolve as leaders, we need to dwell on how good relates to evil, virtue to vice, love to hatred, means to end, sacred to profane. This means we must understand human beings for what they truly are. If leaders sometimes look highly virtuous, it is because they have cleverly concealed their vices. This is again a great skill. We need to learn all attributes of leadership, even those that appear immoral, illegal or vicious.

A leader is generally not more virtuous than most ordinary people. The opposite is usually true. Because people are reluctant to be led by those perceived as evil, a leader expertly creates a façade, behind which he hides all that may appear dirty. This is a difficult art where the leader has to wear two masks, one in public and the other in private—and no one should see the true face of a leader.

You may find some chapters in this book disturbing as they challenge popular notions. For example, the chapter, *Cover Your Evil*, states that leaders must conceal their evil thoughts and deeds and hunt for scapegoats to transfer their evil onto, so as to maintain their clean image. Though unethical, these traits do work for most leaders.

Also, the chapter, *Be an Actor*, claims that leaders need to be great actors. Some readers may question: Why can't leaders be genuine? What is the need to fake our emotions? But then this world, we all know, is not what it should ideally be. Hence, a leader also cannot for all practical purposes match up to what he ideally should be. We can achieve ordinary things of life by being honest and true. However, to achieve extraordinary things, we need to act and exaggerate. In a movie, does the hero ever go about his business in an ordinary fashion, displaying average strength and character? He cannot because people wish to see him as the superman who battles enemies heroically and solves all problems. A leader must likewise fit into the imagination of his followers, however weird and unrealistic those may be. If you don't size up to it, someone else will readily fill the mould.

Certain principles like 'divide and rule' are eternal in the game of leadership, however unethical they may sound. For, if everyone is united, there is probably no need for a leader. Leaders emerge to unite the divisions and counter all opponents. This policy though need not be immoral, if our intentions are right. The logic governing this principle is discussed in the chapter, *Divide and Rule for Success*.

Deception is yet another principle that may appear immoral, but is essential if a leader is to succeed. It's often rated as the most efficient method to bring down your enemy; you can win without firing a single shot. Even if unwilling to deceive, you must still be skilled in the art of deception, for your enemies are bound to use it against you. Knowing can guard you from your deceivers, both within and outside. You can read more in the chapter, *Why Leaders Need to Deceive?*

Aspiring leaders must also understand that leadership is not an easy game because there is no rule for leadership. There is no competitive examination to select the leaders, and there is no minimum qualification to become a leader. When your rivals are using all means to succeed, it would be foolish to fight them only by moral means.

The book also highlights practical methods for developing positive qualities like courage, initiative and team-building. There is a whole section dealing with *Developing Leadership*. We discuss the importance of team-building and complementing strengths to achieve desired results for the organisation. Steps to develop imagination and initiative are extensively illustrated.

Lastly, in the section, *Practising Leadership*, we describe how to be an effective leader in management positions. The chapter, *Managing in Organisation* provides practical steps to manage your bosses, subordinates, competitors and customers. You'll find tested techniques that can improve your performance in the *Decision-making* chapter.

On completing this book, you will gain insights into leadership that is very close to reality as I have unmasked the full story. Knowing the whole truth will best prepare you to become a leader and succeed in your life goals.

PART I

THE NEED FOR LEADERSHIP

1

Who Can Be a Leader?

Before you are a leader, success is all about growing yourself. When you become a leader, success is all about growing others.

—Jack Welch

Managing people is the most difficult science but the easiest art. Even if you have read all the books on management and leadership or graduated from a top management college or attended numerous training courses on leadership development, you could still be very poor in managing people. On the other hand, even if you have read no such books, never been to a management school, had no formal or informal training in man management and leadership, you can still manage people efficiently, provided you understand them.

Leadership is perhaps the only profession where performance matters more than anything else. It really does not matter how you succeed. If you produce results, all means are acceptable.

A cab driver reaches the pearly gates of Heaven. St Peter looks into his Big Book and tells him to pick up the gold staff and silk robe, and proceed onwards into Heaven.

Next in line is a preacher. St Peter looks him up too in his Big Book, furrows his brow and says, 'Ok, we'll let you in, but you take that cloth robe and wooden staff.'

The preacher is shocked and protests, 'But I am a man of the cloth. You gave that cab driver a gold staff and a silk robe. Surely I rate higher than a cabbie!'

St Peter responds matter-of-factly, 'This is Heaven and up here, we are interested in results. When you preached, people slept. When the cabbie drove his taxi, people prayed.'

You need certain inherent qualities to succeed in any field of life. You need high scores to make it to the top engineering colleges or business schools; a strong and flexible body to be a sportsman; much imagination and great command over language to be a writer, and a beautiful face and body, if you wish to be a movie star.

Every field lays down some criteria based on which we know if we are fit to enter that field or not. As far as leadership is concerned, there are no clearly defined criteria or attributes that tell us whether we are leadership material or not. As a result, everyone believes that he or she can be a leader.

This makes leadership the most deceptive game in the world. The only law for leadership is that there is no law. The only rule that a leader follows is that he follows no rule.

Take the case of political leadership. Here too, everyone thinks he can rise to be a leader. Why not? After all, we see all types of people entering politics to lead the country. From film stars to commoners, sportsmen to physically challenged, army generals to junior officials, rich to poor, uneducated to scholars—politics beckons all.

If there is one field in the world where everyone thinks he can succeed, it is politics. Yet, very few go on to be great political leaders. With massive numbers in the running to be a leader, it's a tough battle and success involves much effort.

It's the same story in the business world. You need not be from Harvard, Cambridge, IIT, IIM or another top college to be a leader. Industry and trade heads have sprung from all wakes of life and have varying educational and social backgrounds. However, they do tend to employ top brains from the leading business schools. After all, even Bill Gates finally needs a Satya Nadella.

Academic qualification, you'll find, is important but not essential for leadership. Thomas Edison had only three months of formal schooling and faced deafness since childhood, yet rose to become one of the most prolific inventors and entrepreneurs in history. Edison held 1,093 US patents in his name, and many more in the United Kingdom, France and Germany. Both Bill Gates and Steve Jobs were college dropouts, but grew to be the greatest business leaders of our time. Back in India, we have Dhirubhai Ambani, just a matriculate who came from a poor family and started out selling *bhajias*—fried vegetable dumplings over the weekends to pilgrims in Mount Girnar. The same Dhirubhai later founded India's biggest corporate empire, Reliance Industries that employed thousands, including hundreds of MBAs from top business schools of the world. Another leading business tycoon of today, Sunil Bharti Mittal too began with a small bicycle business in Ludhiana, in partnership with his friend. Mittal over time, went on to form Bharti Telecom Limited, which is now the top telecom company in India, boasting a turnover of several billion dollars and ranked as the third largest telecommunication company in the world in 2014, having over 250 million customers.

Stories of such rise abound. It is not surprising thus, that most people believe they too can strike it big and emerge as great leaders.

Two teachers walking on the road passed by the mansion of the richest businessman in the country. One teacher said to the other, 'If only I can get all the factories of this man along with all his wealth, I can earn more than him.'

'How do you think you can do that,' asked his fellow teacher.

'Look, I shall make as much money as this gentleman is making from all his businesses. And then I shall also give couple of tuitions to add to my income,' replied the beaming teacher.

Such illogical beliefs reign rampant. Hence, everyone tries to become a leader by aping the style of great leaders, hoping to repeat their success stories. However, in reality, so many entrepreneurs who dream of setting up global corporations struggle to even survive in their business. Studies show that less than 20 per cent of the new ventures survive beyond five years.

The Art of Leadership

'To lead yourself, use your head. To lead others, use your heart,' said John Maxwell. 'Always touch a person's heart before you ask him for a hand.' Academic knowledge can strengthen your mind, but may not enrich your heart. Leadership usually comes from the heart as your heart tells you to follow a leader and unite with him and his way of life.

It is easy to manage people when you know them well, and not just superficially. But it is tough to really know people because people rarely expose their intimate self to anyone outside their trusted circle. Also, there is no set formula for working on people, because what works for one person may do just the opposite for another. So the art of leadership is complex and not for all.

And we must not forget that people don't just keep changing, but there are multiple facets to every personality. An abhorred criminal can turn into a saint, and the greatest saint can act like a criminal. For within every person, there resides a criminal and a saint. Leaders thus need to deal with all aspects of a persona and frame perceptions in tune with time and situation.

Leaders and Followers

It is a common belief that people can be broadly divided into two categories: Leaders and followers. One who is not a leader is a follower. Often people take them to be leaders who have a sizable following. But in reality, a leader need not necessarily have followers.

You do not become a leader because people follow you. Rather, people tend to follow you because you have leadership qualities. The journey of leadership often starts alone. Attorney Ward Lamon, the law partner of Abraham Lincoln tells us how Lincoln decided to go alone against popular opinion.

> The lawyers on the bar got together one night and tried Lincoln on the charge of accepting fees, which was lower than the established rates. There was an unstated rule in the bar that a lawyer should extract maximum money from clients. The tribunal was known as 'The Ogmathorial Court'.
>
> Lincoln was found guilty and fined for his awful crime against the pockets of his brothers of the bar. The fine he paid with great good humour, and then kept the crowd of lawyers in uproarious laughter until after midnight.
>
> However, he persisted in his revolt declaring that with his consent his firm should never during its life, or after its dissolution, deserve the reputation enjoyed by those shining lights of the profession, 'Catch them and cheat them.'

Leadership means taking charge of your life, choosing your own path and making yourself responsible for all your actions. Such a person is a leader whether or not such a person is followed by anyone. Douglas MacArthur, the American general and field marshal of the Philippine

Army, who was chief of staff of the United States Army during the 1930s and played a prominent role in the Pacific theatre during World War II, rightly said, 'A true leader has the confidence to stand alone, the courage to make tough decisions and the compassion to listen to the needs of others. He does not set out to be a leader, but becomes one by the equality of his actions and the integrity of his intent.'

As a matter of fact, most leaders have to walk alone on their chosen path as they believe in being on 'the right path', even if at odds with popular belief. Rabindranath Tagore, the Nobel laureate and one of the greatest poets of India too advised people to move alone, in some stage of their lives—*Ekla cholo re*

> If they answer not to thy call, walk alone.
>
> If they are afraid and cower mutely facing the wall,
>
> O thou unlucky one, open thy mind and speak out alone.
>
> If they turn away, and desert you when crossing the wilderness,
>
> O thou unlucky one, trample the thorns under thy tread, and along the blood-lined track, travel alone.
>
> If they do not hold up the light when the night is troubled with storm,
>
> O thou unlucky one, with the thunder flame of pain ignite thy own heart, and let it burn alone.

The journey of leadership mostly starts alone. One has to first lead himself before he can expect others to follow him. If you are unwilling to buy what you are selling, can you expect others to buy it? Leadership is not a game of numbers. It is not about counting the followers behind you. What counts is the development of leadership qualities that pronounce you a leader. When you have these qualities, you are unlikely to be afraid of walking alone and taking decisions that others may not consider prudent or profitable.

Just like a teacher remains a teacher even when he has no student, a leader stays a leader whether or not he has any followers. Similarly, a follower will continue to be a follower even when there is no leader. For example, there are people who follow rituals, self-help books, advice of experts, management principles, scriptures and even mythologies, as if these were the gospel truth. They are followers without leaders.

Just like a student need not have a teacher if he can study from the books directly, a person can follow even in the absence of leaders. You become a follower every time you follow in the footsteps of anyone, whether living or not.

A leader is one who travels the path carved out by him, and he 'leads' himself onward on that path. If his path is good and his goals are desirable, many more may follow him in their desire to achieve the same goal. Hence, followership is the effect of leadership and not its cause.

We usually follow others when we find some benefit in doing so. So a leader must have something of value to offer to his followers. Leadership does not necessarily come with designation, title or post. Take the case of Mullah Nasruddin who led by virtue of his innate abilities, and not the turban that denoted his high post.

> One day an illiterate man came to Mullah Nasruddin with a letter he had received.
>
> 'Mullah Nasruddin, please read out this letter to me.'
>
> Mullah Nasruddin looked at the letter, but could not make out a single word. So he told the man, 'I am sorry, but I can't read this.'
>
> The man cried, 'What a shame, Mullah Nasruddin! You shame the turban you wear.'
>
> Mullah Nasruddin then removed the turban from his head and placed it on the head of the illiterate man and said, 'There, now

you wear the turban. If it makes you knowledgeable, read the letter yourself.'

A Leader Delivers

Leadership is all about producing results. Peter Drucker, the father of management, rightly said, 'It is not whether the answer is right. It is whether it works.' That is why Lincoln allowed General Grant to lead his army even when the general was accused of drinking.

> 'Grant is a drunkard,' asserted powerful and influential politicians to the president at the White House time after time. 'He is not himself half the time; he can't be relied upon, it is a shame to have such a man in command of an army.'
>
> 'So Grant gets drunk, does he?' queried Lincoln, addressing himself to one of the particularly active detractors of the soldier. 'Yes, he does and I can prove it,' was the reply.
>
> 'Well,' returned Lincoln, with the faintest suspicion of a twinkle in his eye, 'You needn't waste your time getting proof; you just find out to oblige me, what brand of whiskey Grant drinks, because I want to send a barrel of it to each one of my generals.'

A leader knows that he shall be judged by the result, and not whether he was following the path which others consider 'right'.

For a leader, the 'right path' is one that produces the desired results.

How can it be otherwise?

Often leaders are considered crazy; sometimes even unethical for they dive into unknown territory and seek absurd, out-of-the-box solutions to life's problems. Steve Jobs, the former CEO and founder of Apple Inc., and one of the greatest leaders and entrepreneurs of modern times, described leaders as 'the round pegs in the square holes'. Jobs went on to say:

Here's to the crazy ones,

the misfits, the rebels, the troublemakers,

the round pegs in the square holes...

the ones who see things differently-

they're not fond of rules....

You can quote them, disagree with them, glorify or vilify them,

but the only thing you can't do is ignore them because they change things...

they push the human race forward,

while some may see them as the crazy ones,

we see genius, because the ones who are crazy enough to think

that they can change the world,

are the ones who do.

Leaders tend to blaze a new trail instead of travelling on the known 'path' as they know that all known paths lead only to known goals. To discover new territories, you have to make your own path, and lead yourself and others on that path.

2

Leader–Follower Dualism

True leadership must have followership. Management styles can vary, but even an autocrat needs people who believe and simply don't follow from fear.
—James Robinson III, RRE Ventures

Leadership is not the privilege of a few as almost everyone has leadership qualities. Just like people have varying degrees of intelligence, height and strength, they also have varying degrees of leadership skills. No one is born a leader; people become leaders by imbibing leadership qualities that they may have gained by following other leaders. It is like how every father is also a son. In fact, it is possible for an individual not to be a father/mother but it is impossible not to be a son/daughter first. Only a son later becomes a father and a student becomes a teacher.

Every person starts as a follower, similar to how every father has first been a son. He learns from leaders who have in turn gained from other leaders. The most successful leaders are usually those who can learn from different leaders, just like the dedicated student who consults many teachers and books for in-depth knowledge. When imbibing leadership qualities, you tend to attract people who too are interested in the same goal. It is similar to students approaching their intelligent classmate to learn from him. Johann Wolfgang Von Goethe, the German writer and statesman said, 'What chance gathers, she easily scatters. A great person attracts great people and knows how to hold them together.'

So as you keep acquiring leadership traits, you are likely to be blessed with more and more followers for they recognise you as more capable. As you grow in life, you may thus find people following you more than they lead you.

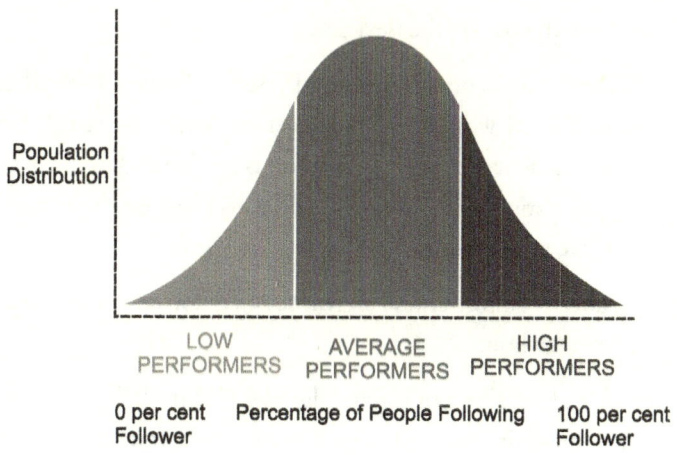

Figure 1: Population distribution of leadership/followership

The bell curve graph in Figure 1 shows that it is rare to find a person who follows everyone or a person who follows no one. Even leaders may follow their followers if required. That is how the equilibrium of leadership-followership is maintained. A good leader does not hesitate to follow someone he finds more qualified than himself. Abraham Lincoln is considered to be the greatest president of the United States, yet he never shied away from learning from his own subordinates.

Old Dennis Hanks was once sent to Washington by these people who wanted to have the men accused of being copperheads released from jail. They thought Old Dennis might have some influence with the president.

President Lincoln heard Dennis' story and then said, 'I will send for Stanton. It is his business.'

Secretary Stanton entered into the room, stormed up and down and said that the men ought to be punished more than they were.

Lincoln sat quietly in his chair and waited for the tempest to subside, and then quietly said to Stanton that he would like to have the papers the next day.

When he had gone, Dennis said, 'Abe, if I was as big and ugly as you are, I would take him over my knee and spank him.' The president replied, 'No, Stanton is an able and valuable man for this nation, and I am glad to bear his anger for the service he can give to the nation.'

A great leader is almost always a great follower for he knows what to learn and from whom.

We are all leaders, albeit in varying degrees, and in different fields of life. It is somewhat like your school mark sheet—your score follows those who scored better and leads those who scored poorer. Even subject-wise, this ranking varies. You rarely find someone who is an absolute winner in all subjects or a complete loser.

Those who are followed by only a few are generally poor performers, while those with a large following are bound to be outstanding performers. They are the leaders. It requires less effort to follow, just as one need not toil much to score low or passing marks. But most of us want to win and this builds in us the desire to perform and lead.

When you are followed by many people, your decision has greater impact, which in turn improves your performance. For those just beginning to lead, it's a long struggle.

Followers are then as important as leaders, for we find that only followers move on to be leaders one day.

An Attitude to Lead is Essential

What makes a leader different from the follower is the attitude to lead. He is not content to simply keep following his leader, but seeks to blaze his own trail. You enrol in a school or college not to remain a student forever, but to acquire knowledge and move on to apply all that you've learnt to rise higher in life.

As has been said earlier, high positions do not make a leader. You could be the top man in your organisation or country and yet be a mere follower. Often heads of states also cannot lead, but are subservient or apathetic to popular will and opinion. Bowing down totally to public opinion or ignoring it altogether, both imply lack of true leadership. A real leader is one who can mould public opinion and march forward.

Leaders who are actually ruled by the people are nothing more than servants. They have been engaged by the public to govern and simply enjoy greater perks and facilities. They follow popular will and are scared of taking any decision that might annoy people. As a result:

- They are unpopular, even when they follow a populist policy.
- They do not command real authority, though they occupy top positions.
- They lack vision despite being perched at a high position.

These highly placed individuals are not free to follow what they believe to be 'right' as they do not have that connect with their people. They may lack the courage to walk alone as it makes them insecure. Many top-rung managers and politicians fall under this category. They merely implement the dictate of their bosses—be they shareholders or the board of directors or even voters in a democracy.

And like most managers, they too praise their bosses in public and curse them in private.

They believe that people's opinions are fixed and cannot be changed. Hence, they change their own conviction and fall in line with the opinion of the people—who are their bosses. And it is this appeasement policy that often makes them very unpopular and invites much ridicule. After all, people are quick to blame their leaders when they fail.

People are simply interested in the betterment of their lives, and they want their leaders to do the same for them, just like we expect our servants to serve us. In such cases, the followers often act as leaders and make leaders follow them, especially when leaders lack conviction and courage. In this contest between leaders and followers, where each tries to dominate the other, it may become difficult to judge who leads and who follows.

A leader does not need to be in a commanding position to lead. He can be at the lowest level of the hierarchy and yet be followed by even the senior-most people.

> General Grant, pacing up and down the docks of city point, puffed his cigar in violation of the rules.
>
> A sentry on duty approached him and let it be known that it was against the rules to smoke there.
>
> 'Are these your orders?' the general asked.
>
> 'Yes sir,' the sentry was courteous, but firm.
>
> 'They are very good orders, sir!' said Grant, as he threw the cigar into the water.

A leader must take responsibility for all his actions and not blame anyone for his problems. The follower, on the other hand, is always in search of a scapegoat or a miracle worker who can solve his problems.

That is why leaders and followers complement each other. A leader is one who is willing to take on responsibility of not only his own failures but also that of his followers. Arnold H Glasow, an American humourist said wisely, 'A good leader takes a little more than his share of the blame, a little less than his share of the credit.'

3

The Myths of Leadership

Effective leadership is not about making speeches or being liked; leadership is defined by results not attributes.

—Peter F Drucker

There is no dearth of books on leadership. There are thousands of management gurus who claim they can transform anyone into a leader. Warren Bennis, an American scholar, organisational consultant and author, widely regarded as a pioneer in the field of leadership studies says, 'The most dangerous leadership myth is that leaders are born— that there is a genetic factor to leadership. That's nonsense. In fact, the opposite is true. Leaders are made rather than born.'

The business of making anyone a leader is a great and profitable one. There are so many quick fix solutions available off-the-shelf from known experts in this field. Many get swayed by the charisma of motivational speakers who promise to turn every man into a leader. But most end up disappointed as these quick fixes fail to produce the desired result. Take the case of this CEO who claimed to have a ready solution for running any organisation.

A person had just been hired as the new head of a global corporation. The outgoing CEO met him privately and presented him three numbered envelopes.

He said, 'Open these when you run up against a problem you don't think you can solve.'

Initially, all went well. But few months later, the company's performance went on a downslide and the new CEO did not know what to do. So he opened the first envelope and read the message: 'Blame your predecessor.'

He quickly called a press conference and held his predecessor responsible for all the ills in the company. His excuse was accepted and soon the company stock was on the rise again. With the company back on track, people developed confidence in the new CEO. However, as time passed, the company hit rough weather again. It faced serious production issues and the sales started declining.

So he opened the second envelope, which had the message: 'Reorganise.'

He thus began to reorganise, transferring executives from one place to another, effecting more changes till the company came out of the red and began posting profits again. After a few years, the company fell on difficult times yet again. It was time for the CEO to open the third envelope.

The message was: 'Prepare three envelopes.'

Such quick fix formulas and leadership lessons abound, but they do not amount to much. These formulas are nothing but myths, which contain only half-truths. The entire story is never told. However, the unsaid bit comes to forefront the moment one starts practising these leadership mantras in real life. So it is better to get a complete picture in advance rather than learning it the hard way.

Leadership Myth 1: Leaders Should Be Good Listeners

'Of all the skills of leadership, listening is the most valuable and one of the least understood,' said Peter Nulty, who wrote for *Fortune* magazine for more than twenty years and worked as communications specialist at McKinsey & Co. 'Most captains of industry listen only sometimes, and they remain ordinary leaders. But few, the great ones, never stop listening. That's how they get word, before anyone else, of unseen problems and opportunities.'

There is no doubt that listening is an important leadership skill. Yet, we must know when to listen, whom to listen to and how much to listen. It is a myth that listening is always good or that every great leader is a listener. When we listen to someone's problems, the problems tend to become ours too. Perhaps, even psychiatrists should be careful and guard themselves against too much listening!

> Two psychiatrists are having a conversation. One is much older than the other, but looks to be in great shape. In contrast, his colleague appears extremely exhausted.
>
> 'I don't understand,' remarks the younger psychiatrist, 'how you can listen to all those half-crazy patients all day long and not be affected by it.'
>
> 'Who listens to them?' replies the older psychiatrist, as he takes out his energy spheres.

A person who confides in you usually expects that you will fix his problem or at least help him solve it. If after hearing his problem, you do nothing, he is likely to get even more frustrated and angry since he has gained nothing even after baring his private self to you. He may also worry that you can misuse your privileged position to exploit him.

> A group of psychiatrists were attending a convention. Four of them decided to leave, and walked out together.
>
> One said to the other three, 'People are always coming to us

with their guilt and fears, but we have no one that we can go to when we have problems.'

The others agreed.

Then one said, 'Since we are all professionals, why don't we take some time right now to hear each other out?'

The other three agreed.

The first then confessed, 'I have an uncontrollable desire to kill my patients.'

The second psychiatrist said, 'I love expensive things and so I look for ways to cheat my patients out of their money in order to buy all the things I want.'

The third followed with, 'I'm involved in drug dealing, and often get my patients to sell them for me.'

The fourth psychiatrist then confessed, 'I know I'm not supposed to, but no matter how hard I try, I can't keep a secret.'

If leaders do nothing after listening to people's problems, they lose the respect of their followers. This is because, as a leader, they failed to deliver on expectations that arose when the follower got a sympathetic hearing.

If a leader actually helps in problem-solving, his follower is happy. But then others also start speaking their minds and hope to get his help in tiding over their problems. The leader might thus get tied up in solving miscellaneous issues of his people rather than achieving the goals of his organisation. His performance is likely to suffer then, which in turn erodes the support of his followers. Bill Cosby, an American actor, author, television producer, musician and activist has wisely said, 'I don't know the key to success, but the key to failure is trying to please everybody.' Listening to everybody in an effort to please them often leads to failure. Those, whose problems do not get solved, develop a negative attitude towards their leader as they wonder why they were ignored. So you must identify whom to listen to, when to listen and how much to listen.

Leadership Myth 2: Leaders Should Be Compassionate

Love and compassion are considered to be amongst the greatest virtues of leaders. You are advised to be always kind and compassionate towards your team. You should appreciate their work and not condemn them for their failures. Henry Ward Beecher, a clergyman and social reformer said, 'Compassion will cure more sins than condemnation.' Yet, it is also a fact that there are many who exploit this compassion.

> It was pouring and a big puddle formed in front of the pub. A ragged old man stood there with a rod, hanging a string into the puddle.
>
> A curious gentleman walked over to him and asked what he was doing.
>
> 'Fishing,' the old man said simply.
>
> 'Poor old fool,' the gentleman thought, and invited the ragged old man to a dinner in a five-star hotel.
>
> While they ate their lavish dinner, just to strike up a conversation the gentleman asked, 'And how many have you caught?'
>
> 'You're the tenth,' the old man answered.

So for leaders, compassion can sometimes be a weakness rather than a strength. When you are compassionate, you may find that the productivity of your team goes down. That's because people don't tend to take you seriously, knowing that they shall not be punished or admonished when they don't put in the required effort. Your compassion is taken for granted and people simply keep expecting more. Dissatisfied with what they have gained, they are prone to cribbing about what they missed.

Also, you cannot be compassionate to everyone and fulfil all their expectations. For example, when you promote someone or award them for their good work, the rest feel hurt and discriminated against. They are likely to label you unjust and biased. You may get condemned even when your decisions were fair and selfless.

A saint or monk can afford to be compassionate to all, but a leader or boss cannot always be kind. He may soon be without a job himself if he is unduly compassionate, and chances are, no one would show him any compassion then.

Leadership Myth 3: Leaders Must Have High Integrity

There is no leadership book that does not mention integrity as the greatest virtue of a leader. Maria Razumich-Zec, the regional vice president, USA East Coast, The Peninsula Hotels, said, 'Your reputation and integrity are everything. Follow through on what you say you're going to do. Your credibility can only be built over time and is built from the history of your words and actions.'

Who can even suggest that integrity should not be the greatest virtue of the leader? We hear that leaders walk their talk, they speak the truth and always fulfil their promises. At least, all leaders claim so. Who, in business or politics, can truly be called honest? It is another matter that some people may be too clever and manage to avoid the law. But their reputations are well-known.

> A man wanted to know which career he should choose for his son. So he put a Bible, a dollar and a bottle of whisky on the table, and slipped behind a curtain. He thought that if the son picked up the Bible, he would be fit to become a priest, if he chose the dollar, he would make a good businessman, and if he opted for the bottle of whiskey, he might become a criminal.
>
> The youth entered the room and saw the things. He thought for a while. Then he tucked the Bible under his arm, slipped the dollar into his pocket and took in a generous dose of whisky.

'Oh my god!' exclaimed the man, 'It looks like he is perfect to be a politician.'

Mark Twain was right when he said, 'Honesty is the best policy, when there is money in it.' Integrity and honesty can be virtues only in an ideal situation and when others are honest too. What if you are writing in an exam and it is for a job which you desperately need? The instructors are lenient and let everyone copy from books and each other. In this situation, if you stick to your principles, you may not stand any chance of success, even if you are extraordinarily intelligent.

While leaders can choose to be relatively honest, there is no way they can be absolutely honest, when others are dishonest. Leaders who refuse to compromise on their honesty at all, may feel satisfied about following their principle, but are unlikely to succeed much.

They can be honest with their core team, but can they afford to be honest with their rivals and enemies?

Leadership Myth 4: Leaders persevere

Hard work and perseverance are said to be the touchstone of successful leaders. People are advised to keep on trying till they succeed. Who has not heard of the great inventor Thomas Edison, who failed 10,000 times before he discovered the light bulb? Even in his failure he saw a lining of success, for he said, 'I have not failed. I've just found 10,000 ways that won't work.' But unless you are blessed with Edison's creativity and the heart to suffer as many failures, you may get demoralised by such repeated failures.

In reality, it is difficult to digest even a single defeat, while our morale is boosted with each success. Only when there is a mix of success and failure, we can take defeat lightly. A success is like a credit in the 'confidence account' while each failure is a debit. The greater the success, more is the deposit. Similarly, greater the failure, more is the debit. Only if you have deposited enough successes in your account, can you withstand a string of failures. Else, you may become bankrupt, depressed and emotionally broken.

Secondly, we must also ask ourselves—why work so hard? The great leaders are not the ones who work very hard, but they are the ones who are smart and efficient. Bill Gates said, 'I choose a lazy person to do a hard job because a lazy person will find an easy way to do it.'

In reality, most people succeed not just because of their perseverance, but because of innovation, and the fact that they enjoy their job. If Edison learned 10,000 different methods of not making an electric bulb, it was because he loved his job. He was learning something new with every experiment. Innovation can occur only when we have time to relax and ponder over the problem.

Conclusion: Avoid quick fixes

It has been explained through examples that there are no quick fix mantras for leadership. There are no universal principles that work in all situations, with all people and all the time. Rather, principles that work must be used at the right place, in the right situation and at the right time. And no principle has a permanent place in life. Just like you need to sleep after a hard day's work, you also need to get back to work after having a good night's sleep. The two are complementary: Sleep rejuvenates you for work, whereas working hard ensures good sleep.

If some principles of leadership appeal to us or have become more saleable, it is because more people are using the opposite principle, which is perhaps instinctive and natural and thus, need not be learned. Acting on instinct often produces quick results, but if we do not temper instinct with reason, there is imbalance in our life.

We need to balance the opposing principles and not adopt one as superior to the other. If integrity is considered a virtue, it may be because most people lack integrity. Also, as only a few succeed in their pursuits, some may link failure with a lack of integrity. But this is not fully true.

When you reason it out, you might conclude that honest people are more likely to fail and the dishonest rise faster. Other management myths like good listening, being compassionate and perseverance too get busted the same way.

A great leader is one who uses the opposite principles with dexterity, as his in-depth knowledge makes him aware of the fundamental principles that govern people and relationships.

The leadership qualities discussed here or taught by management gurus are not without purpose, as these qualities are counter-intuitive. These are like the 'thumb rules' providing broad guidelines on particular subjects. Typically, rules of thumb develop as a result of practice and experience rather than scientific research or theory.

Thumb rules provide general principles without giving reasons or the fundamental principles from which these rules have been derived. For example, in order to maintain good health, people are advised to avoid high-calorie, high-fat diets and regularly exercise. This rule seems to be true for most of us who tend to be overweight and not very physically active. Yet, this is not a universal formula and cannot be applied to manual workers, like labourers or underweight people, for whom just the opposite may be true. Labourers need not exercise and also we must know that no diet can be ideal for everyone. Similarly, there is no thumb rule that can be used universally by all leaders in all situations. Leaders need to understand the fundamental principles behind these thumb rules in order to use them well and let their intuition guide them on the right approach each time.

4

Why Must You Aspire to Be a Leader?

In this world, those who desire only wealth are of the lowest order; those who desire wealth and respect are of the middle order; the people of the highest order are those who desire honour and respect.

—Chanakya

It is not easy to become a leader. Most people do not achieve the level of leadership they aspire as leadership is an extremely competitive arena. Most of the times, leaders are in the news for the wrong reasons as media is quick to highlight even their tiniest fault and often, blows it out of proportion. The public too derives vicarious satisfaction from leader-bashing as it itself could not become one of them. Sometimes, people develop the opinion that it is not worth becoming a leader. Let us therefore understand what we achieve by becoming a leader.

1. Confidence

Leaders are confident people for they choose their own path. Taking on the risk that comes with new territory, they move forward employing their intuition and judgment. They, thus, learn to bear responsibility for both their successes and failures and are not prone to blame others. Instead of cursing their circumstances and people who created the problem, they learn to view issues as opportunities and gain confidence from their experiences. Their knowledge is real as it is practical. As Einstein said, 'The only source of knowledge is experience.' Even in adverse situations, they stay mostly unperturbed as experience makes them confident of overcoming all problems.

2. Honour

Leaders are honoured by the society since they add value to it. Harry S Truman said, 'Men make history and not the other way around. In periods where there is no leadership, society stands still. Progress occurs when courageous, skilful leaders seize the opportunity to change things for the better.' In times of crisis, people are always looking for leaders and saviours. This is amply reflected in movies, where the hero usually arrives to fight the villains for the common man and helps them lead a better life. In Gita, Lord Krishna said, 'Whenever and wherever there is a decline in dharma, O descendant of Bharata, and a predominant rise of evil, at that time I descend Myself.'

Leaders help individuals and the society in general, which in turn bestows on them great honour. Many great leaders like Buddha and Gandhi were deified. Others like Napoleon, Stalin, Mao, Churchill and Roosevelt are honoured even today. Great leaders are remembered even after they are no more. Benjamin Franklin said, 'If you would not be forgotten as soon as you are dead and rotten, either write things worth reading or do things worth writing.'

3. Power

Leaders acquire power due to the support of a large number of willing followers. One Gandhi managed to galvanise millions of Indians and one Hitler ensured that Germany defeated France in a matter of days. A leader is the epitome of power and kings were traditionally worshipped as God in many nations. They were believed to represent God on Earth, as they were all-powerful.

When you are a leader, you can perform and achieve the desired results as you wield so much power.

4. Success

People become leaders because they deliver results. They perform consistently and produce the results they have promised. Hence, they are valued by every organisation and the society as people trust their words and believe that they will deliver. People seek results, not explanations for failure. Offering even a thousand reasons for failure cannot convert it into a success, whereas the latter needs no explanation. As leaders perform, they rise up the organisational ladder fast to occupy the top post.

5. Wealth

Dale Carnegie in his classic, *How to Win Friends and Influence People*, states the role of leadership in generating wealth.

> The highest paid personnel in engineering are frequently not those who know the most about engineering. One can, for example, hire mere technical ability in engineering, accountancy, architecture or any other profession at nominal salaries. But the person who has technical knowledge plus the ability to express ideas, to assume leadership and to arouse enthusiasm among people—that person is headed for higher earning power.

Leaders are the best paid in any organisation. If they choose to turn into entrepreneurs, they make big money. Leaders like Bill Gates and Steve Jobs could earn billions of dollars while still in their twenties. Napoleon and Alexander grew extremely powerful and wealthy at early ages by virtue of their leadership. Getting to lead is perhaps the best compensation one can get.

Work at Becoming a Leader

Leaders usually acquire what is sought by most people. No wonder then that there is tremendous competition to secure a leadership role in any organisation. We must all try to become leaders—perform efficiently and fulfil aspirations. Criticism is but a small price for success. Elbert Green Hubbard, the American writer, publisher, artist and philosopher said:

> The man who is anybody and who does anything is surely going to be criticised, vilified and misunderstood. That is part of the penalty for greatness and every great man understands it; and understands too, that it is no proof of greatness. The final proof of greatness lies in being able to endure continuously without resentment. To avoid criticism do nothing, say nothing, be nothing.

However, I am sure that even if you do nothing, say nothing and be nothing, there will still be many who will criticise you. It is much better to be criticised for success than be condemned for failures because success rids you of the many miseries of life.

5

Transform into a Leader

There can be no power without mystery. There must always be a 'something' which others can't altogether fathom, which puzzles them, stirs them and rivets their attention.

—Charles de Gaulle

Like the magnet, a leader has great qualities to attract and repel. His magnetic personality draws people, who in time, develop similar leadership qualities. Those repulsed by a leader usually have opposite traits. Also, a leader generally attracts another potential leader.

A leader may sometimes force people to work against their will, but then he also charms them to give their best. Take the case of Hitler who was known to be a dictator but had a magnetic personality. The SS-Brigade leader Julius Schreck recalls,

> Major journeys are undertaken by The Leader only in an open vehicle, which he refuses to close even if it rains in the course of an official visit. To the advice of his entourage, his only response is always, 'As long as the SA and the other groups have to stand in the rain, we can get wet as well.'

A leader can thus convert people. To understand how leaders transform others, let us see how an ordinary piece of iron gets transformed into a powerful magnet.

Transformation of Iron to Magnet

An ordinary piece of iron does not have any power to attract or repel. Its power is limited to that power of any material to attract other material objects, that is, only by gravitational force, which is infinitely smaller than the magnetic attraction.

A piece of iron is divided into small domains with all atoms aligned in the same direction. These domains, however, are distributed in a random manner and hence, the net magnetism is zero. When this ordinary piece of iron is brought into a strong magnetic field, all the domains get aligned in one direction and the iron is converted into a strong magnet having the power to attract other pieces of iron.

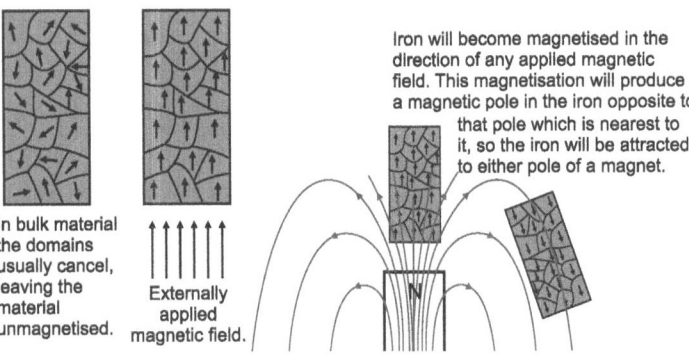

We are like ordinary iron whose desires are scattered in all directions. We wish to do everything and want to be everything. In our quest for getting everything, we often end up getting nothing. A leader with his magnetic personality aligns our desires in one direction, transforming in the process all those who come in close contact.

In transforming large numbers, great leaders can create many more leaders. They mimic the magnet that can transform unlimited number of iron pieces into magnet without losing any of its own magnetic properties.

> The occasion was the laying of the foundation stone of Banaras Hindu University in India. There were many prominent people present in the meeting, including those who had donated to the university fund. When Gandhi spoke of the shame India was suffering under foreign rule and went on to attack first the British Raj and then the princes, one by one, the princes rose and left the meeting in protest. Then the officers of the British Raj left. Gandhi, however, continued to speak even when the chairman had left. Only when Gandhi observed that the chair was empty did he decide to conclude his speech.
>
> Gandhi lost the chairman and the princes that day, but won the heart of a young eleven-year-old boy. Years later, this boy left everything to become a follower of Gandhi and went on to become the prime minister of India.
>
> His name was Lal Bahadur Shastri.

Mahatma Gandhi created a breed of leaders who were upright, nationalist and selfless—like himself. Many of them later occupied top positions in the government of independent India. However, there were thousands who never occupied any high positions, but continued the Gandhian way of life, bequeathing their Gandhian principles to the next generation.

A single leader transforms thousands of ordinary people into leaders through his magnetic appeal, that makes people discover their own selves and recognise their leadership potential.

PART II

DILEMMA OF LEADERS

1

Can an End Justify the Means

A means can be justified only by its end. But the end, in its turn, needs to be justified.

                    −Leon Trotsky, Their Morals and Ours

The debate on the end and means is not new. Whether an end justifies the means or not is the eternal philosophical and spiritual question. Gandhi believed that the end does not validate the means, and that means and end are one and the same thing. However, people tend to disagree. In movies, we often see the hero breaking all rules only to achieve his end, and people applaud his endeavour. Machiavelli therefore advises, 'For that reason, let a prince have the credit of conquering and holding his state, the means will always be considered honest, and he will be praised by everybody.'

The path and the goal may be different realities, yet they are not independent of each other. In order to arrive at a particular goal, there may be many paths, and no path can be termed superior or inferior as long as you can reach your goal. Sometimes, the smallest path—a straight line—may not exist or may not be the most convenient one. Often, the longer or curvaceous path turns out to be more suitable. And sometimes, you have to make your own path.

> Nasruddin heard that the king had sent out a committee incognito, seeking candidates suitable to be *qazis*—judges. Nasruddin took to walking around with an old fishing net flung across his shoulder. When the members of the committee reached his village, the net drew their attention. They questioned him about it.
>
> 'Oh, I carry this net with me to remind me of my humble past—I was a poor fisherman,' explained Nasruddin. The committee was impressed and in due time, Nasruddin got nominated to be a *qazi*.
>
> Shortly afterwards, the king's representatives met Nasruddin again and noticed that the net was gone.
>
> 'Where is the net, Nasruddin?' they asked.
>
> 'Well, you don't need the net after the fish is caught, do you?' replied Nasruddin.

In *Mahabharata*, all the great Kaurava warriors were killed because the Pandavas had used evil means, turning the war unethical. But imagine, if only fair means would have been employed, the Pandavas would have lost the war. The result would have been the victory of the Kauravas. *Adharma*—unrighteousness would have won. That would have been far more dangerous for the world than the victory of righteousness through unfair means.

You have to decide if a 'good end by evil means' is better than 'good means that lead to an evil end'. This is a difficult decision, but unavoidable in the real world. It is tough to win fairly when your opponent is using all types of unfair means.

This conflict between end and means remains the greatest dilemma for every leader.

Are Ends Same as the Means?

'He who chooses the beginning of a road, chooses the place it leads to. It is the means that determine the end,' said the American Pastor Harry Emerson Fosdick. If we closely analyse the events of the world, we find that most evil acts in this world were perpetuated in the garb of a good end. Whether, it was the Soviet Revolution where the czar was assassinated with his entire family and the Soviet Communist Party replaced them with a regime which was even more brutal. Or the French Revolution that overthrew the emperor only to bring in Napoleon later. Even Hitler fought the war in the name of equality and justice.

Wilhelm Reich, an Austrian psychoanalyst and one of the most radical figures in the history of psychiatry wrote:

> You think the end justifies the means, however vile. I tell you: The end is the means by which you achieve it. Today's step is tomorrow's life. Great ends can't be attained by base means. You've proved that in all your social upheavals. The meanness and inhumanity of the means make you mean and inhuman, and make the end unattainable.

Means affect the end because there is an interconnection between thoughts and acts. You are what your thoughts are. If your thoughts are good, your deeds shall naturally be good. But if your thoughts are evil, you soon fall into the trap of evil. Thoughts and actions are interconnected like our soul and body. The two coexist and make each other.

Just like thoughts affect actions, actions too affect thoughts. If you have chosen evil means, your thoughts will turn evil too. Instead of thinking about the good end, you concern yourself more with how to defend yourself in case you are caught in your evil act. Your focus shifts to your immediate future, far away from the good end that you set out to achieve.

Thus, the evil act gradually transforms you from a good man to an evil one. In time, your eyes get clouded with so much evil that you can't see any goodness and nobility, for goodness is now your enemy and you must fight good people to complete your acts. And when you fight the good, you must ally yourself with evil, as no good person will battle with goodness. Thereafter, you arrive at the crossroads, where even if you wish, the evil shall not leave you. It is too late. On the path of evil, there is no place for honesty and integrity.

> A couple was over speeding, when they were stopped by the traffic cop.
>
> Cop: Sir, you realise that you were speeding?
>
> Husband: I am sorry, officer, I didn't know.
>
> Wife: What the hell. That's a lie. I have been telling him for miles!
>
> Husband: Shut up! No one is talking to you!
>
> Cop: Okay then, did you know that your license plate has expired?
>
> Husband: No, officer. I didn't know.
>
> Wife: He's again telling a lie! I've been telling him for months!
>
> Husband: Shut the hell up! Nobody is talking to you!
>
> Cop then walks over to the wife's side and says, 'Ma'am, does he always talk to you this way?'
>
> Wife: No. Only when he's drunk.

The marriage between good and evil does not last long. When you follow evil, it is a one way traffic. A good man can turn evil anytime, but it is difficult for an evil person to become good again as the world is not ready to forgive easily. Just like water flows down naturally, man too falls easily and finds it tough to rise again. You may have done a thousand good things and that one evil act, but the world is most likely to remember that wrong act and punish you for it. A criminal gets no respite on account of his past good deeds. When caught, he must pay for every act of crime. This is the rule of the world.

Do Ends Actually Exist?

In real life, every end is actually a beginning for another end. Hence, there are actually no ends; each end is nothing but a means to the next end. Therefore, if the end is good, it implies that the means are also good.

It is true that you have to keep the destination in mind while selecting a path. However, it is nearly impossible to find a straight path. When Martin Luther King Junior says, 'Means we use must be as pure as the ends we seek,' he talks about a world, which is straight and plain. In reality, when you wish to reach somewhere, the path is almost never straight.

A wise man thus seeks not a straight path, but one that is the shortest or most convenient. The idea is to reach your goal comfortably and quickly rather than wasting your time in finding, 'Which is the straightest path?'

If you are determined to follow only the straight path, you may not reach anywhere as the first hurdle can check your journey. You might try to justify your non-arrival by pointing out that the path was not straight. But people are unlikely to buy your argument for they are interested only in arriving at the destination. You might become a great philosopher or thinker by pursuing your principles, but not a great leader, as no one follows a failed man. Your ego may be satisfied but your mission would remain unaccomplished.

On the contrary, if you are fighting for a noble end without any hatred or self interest, even your ignoble acts may be ignored.

> Imam Ali, son-in-law of Prophet Mohammad and an invincible warrior, was once engaged in a battle. When Ali pointed his sword at the opponent's throat, he spat on his face. Ali then said to the man 'Go away, taking your life is wrong for me'.
>
> The enemy enquired why he was being released.
>
> Ali replied, 'When you spat on my face, I felt hurt, and if I kill you now, it shall be for my own sake, and not for the sake of Truth. Taking your life will now make me a murderer.'

Why Leaders Get Criticised

The actions of a leader are always criticised by scholars as well as common men. A scholar has no obligation to produce result, so he is free to rebuke leaders for not sticking to noble means. Common men envy leaders for their position and power, thus feeling happy in vilifying them to pull them down to their own levels.

A true leader is responsible for his followers who have reposed their faith in his leadership. If an ordinary man fails, it is a personal failure. But when a leader fails, he shatters the entire ideologies, principles and morale of all those who followed him. The impact is much bigger and stakes are higher. Hence, a leader is expected to sacrifice his personal views for the good of his followers. Those who consider their ideals to be supreme, thus, rarely become leaders.

Therefore, intellectuals are rarely successful as leaders. They are so trapped in their ideals that they cannot venture out in the real world to win and lead. Can an army win a war if the general is extremely kind, compassionate and good?

Even Gandhi, the greatest pacifist, a preacher of non-violence and one of the greatest leaders of twentieth century supported war when there was a need to choose the lesser evil. Louis Fischer writes in his biography, *Mahatma Gandhi–His Life & Times*, 'The day after war's beginning, Gandhi pledged publicly that he would not embarrass the British government. He would also lend moral support to England and her allies; even one who disapproved of war should distinguish between aggressor and defender.'

A wise leader knows that ends are more important than means. It does not imply that leaders have to necessarily travel on an evil path to achieve noble ends, but if they have to traverse that route for some time, they would not hesitate to do it for a noble end. This is the ultimate sacrifice a leader must make. For a leader, there is nothing good or evil; he tries to stay above these distinctions. He aims only at the result and achieves them for his followers—by all means, be it good or evil.

2

The Connect between Good and Evil

If only it were all so simple! If only there were evil people somewhere insidiously committing evil deeds, and it were necessary only to separate them from the rest of us and destroy them. But the line dividing good and evil cuts through the heart of every human being. And who is willing to destroy a piece of his own heart?

—Aleksandr Solzhenitsyn

Evil implies all that is morally wrong. Good stands for all that is right and beneficial for the society. Good and evil are like light and darkness. In general, all wish to be good and perform only good deeds in their lives. Why would anyone want to do anything evil when it is considered a crime in this world and sin in the other world? Yet, in reality, the world seems to be deeply submerged in evil and we see it all around us.

The first question that comes to our mind is, which of the two—good or evil, is the natural trait of man? It is important to know this because if one is natural, the other becomes artificial. A natural trait can be effortlessly pursued whereas the artificial can be deliberately avoided. Anatole France, the French poet and journalist remarked, 'Nature has no principles. She makes no distinction between good and evil.' It requires wisdom of the sages to understand that good and evil are woven together in the fabric of life. The American poet Joaquin Miller explains this in his poem:

> In men whom men condemn as ill
> I find so much of goodness still,
> In men whom men pronounce divine
> I find so much of sin and blot,
> I do not dare to draw a line
> Between the two, where God has not.

We can see that the concepts of good and evil are interdependent and woven together.

Induction Effect of Good and Evil

According to the Genesis, the fall of man is attributed to eating the fruit from the tree of 'Good and Evil'. This phenomenon has been described as the 'Original Sin', which saw Adam and Eve thrown out from the Garden of Eden to suffer in this world.

To understand why the knowledge of Good and Evil is considered the Original Sin of man, we must delve in the origin of Good and Evil. When a person transforms from good to evil or vice versa, the phenomenon mimics electrostatic induction, which is used to charge a piece of article temporarily.

A normal piece of matter has equal number of positive and negative electric charges in each part. Hence, it bears no 'net' electric charge. As shown in Figure 1, when a charged object is brought near an uncharged, electrically conducting object, such as a piece of metal, the force of the nearby charge causes a separation of these charges. For example, if a positive charge is brought near the object, the electrons in the metal will be attracted towards it and move to the side of the object facing it. This leaves an unbalanced positive charge on the opposite end of the object. This results in a region of negative charge on the object nearest to the external charge, and a region of positive charge on the part away from it. These are called induced charges.

As there is only a redistribution of the charges on the body of the object, the net charge of the object remains zero. This induction effect is reversible; if the nearby charge is removed, the attractions between the positive and negative internal charges cause them to intermingle again.

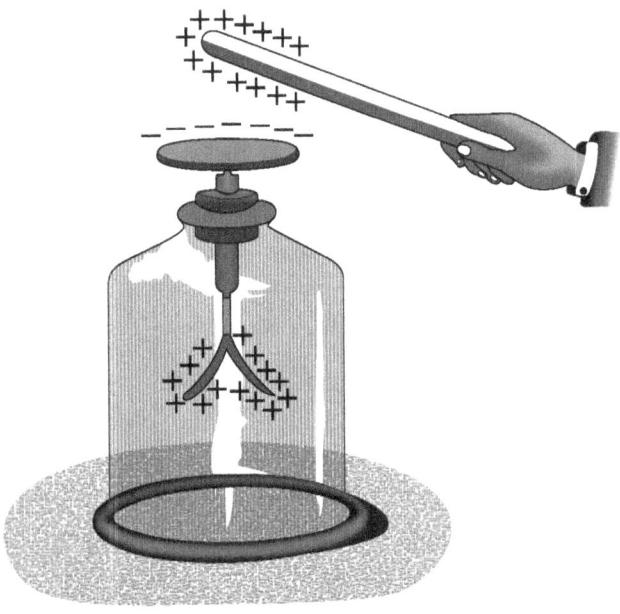

Figure 1: Electrostatic induction of charges

A similar phenomenon is also observed in magnetic substances. A piece of iron is magnetised when it is brought near a strong magnet, and gets converted into a permanent magnet. However, it simultaneously develops both poles—north and south, on the opposite ends of the magnet, which are equal but opposite to each other.

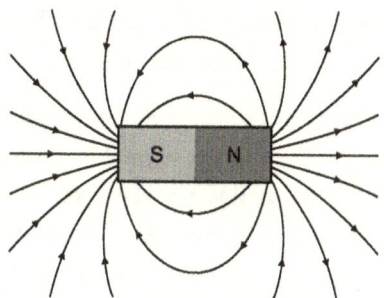

Figure 2: The North and South polarities of a magnet

The principles governing electric charges and magnetism seem to reflect in human beings too. As children, we are all innocent about good and evil. However, as we grow older, elders inculcate in us the sense of right and wrong—good and evil. The society and elders induce us to be good by putting in us the fear of evil or by promising us great things in life if we follow the good path and do good deeds. We are also threatened with punishments if we commit any wrong.

Yet, as demonstrated by the experiment of electrostatic induction, equal and opposite evil is created as soon as good is induced in us. This evil may remain hidden in our heart. Though we may not express it overtly, yet it is always present inside.

The opposite is also true.

When evil is externally induced in us by circumstances or company, an equal good is created inside our heart and we develop a craving to do good things in life. The great American leader, Abraham Lincoln had rightly said, 'It has been my experience that folks who have no vices have very few virtues.'

How can the vices be the source of virtues?

The only way to become free from evil is to shun all good. That is also the attitude of saints. For the same reason, those seeking Nirvana or *Mukti*—enlightenment, are advised to shun all deeds, whether good or evil. It is because good is embedded in evil and evil is contained in each act of goodness. This is clearly said in *Tao Te Ching*:

> When the world knows beauty as beauty, ugliness arises
> When it knows good as good, evil arises.
> The Tao doesn't take sides;
> It gives birth to both good and evil.
> The Master doesn't take sides;
> He welcomes both saints and sinners.

Leaders are not neutral—as being neutral implies being ineffective. They are charged with all good intentions and are ready to do all good deeds. Yet, they also understand that good acts can't be done without evil actions.

Understanding Good and Evil

When we define something as good, the opposite becomes evil and vice versa. If we say that love is good, hatred automatically turns evil. But in some cases, even hatred can be good and there love turns evil—if it is against injustice.

What we consider evil or sinful like wrath, greed, pride, lust and envy are not unnatural to men. We all get angry; we all want more from life. Who does not behave lazily at times? How can it be wrong to have pride in what we are and what we do? Lust is also a biological need, which is responsible for procreation and sustenance of the human race. Even envy cannot be termed evil for it also prompts you to do better.

Therefore, what is often termed evil may actually be something which is natural and important for us. As American guitarist, Dave Mustaine pointed out, 'The *Bible* and several other self-help or enlightenment books cite the Seven Deadly Sins. They are: Pride, greed, lust, envy, wrath, sloth and gluttony. That pretty much covers everything that we do, that is sinful...or fun for that matter.'

It is not possible to take these traits out of your life, unless you are willing to take life out of you. Who knew this truth better than the great British leader, Winston Churchill, who was not only a chainsmoker, but also known for his intemperance in drinking.

> It was towards the close of World War II, and Churchill was visited by a delegation of the Temperance League. And one of the ladies there firmly chastised him, saying, 'Mr Prime Minister, I've heard of all the brandy you have drunk since the war began, and heard that if it were poured into this room, it would come up all the way to your waist.'
>
> And Churchill looked dolefully down at the floor, and then at his waist, then up to the ceiling and said, 'Ah, yes madam, so much accomplished and so much more left to do.'

'Great leaders are not defined by the absence of weakness, but rather by the presence of clear strengths,' says the German American Journalist John Zenger. Instead of worrying over their weaknesses, leaders prefer to focus on their strengths. Management consultant and author, Peter Drucker in his book *The Effective Executive* advises leaders and executives to accept weaknesses along with strengths.

> Whoever tries to place a man or staff in an organisation to avoid weakness will end up at best with mediocrity. The idea that there are 'well-rounded' people, people who have only strengths and no weaknesses...is a prescription for mediocrity, if not for incompetence. Strong people always have strong weaknesses too. Where there are peaks, there are valleys. And no one is strong in many areas. Measured against the universe of human knowledge, experience and abilities, even the greatest genius would have to be rated a total failure. There is no such thing as a 'good man'. Good for what is the question.

Broadly speaking, goodness implies selflessness, whereas evil stands for selfish acts which benefit only the doer. Yet, the two are interconnected as it is impossible to work for the society without first helping the self. Let us take the example of American retail giant, WalMart and see how people perceive this company:

> Between 1997 and 2001, the company's stock value increased by over 500 per cent, rising by 70 per cent in 1997 alone. Today, with $288 billion in annual revenues—more than Switzerland's GDP and over $10 billion in profits, WalMart is the world's largest corporation according to the 2005 Fortune 500 list. It operates over 5,000 stores worldwide and employs over 1.6 million people to 1.3 million in the United States alone.
>
> That growth has been accompanied by two distinct kinds of perceptions among the public. On one hand, WalMart has been celebrated for its business innovations, which have set a new global standard for efficiency. On the other, it has been condemned for its hard-charging business practices. One of the most prominent attacks came last November, when filmmaker Robert Greenwald released *WalMart: The High Cost of Low Price*, a documentary that excoriated the company for its approach to unions, independent retailers, outsourcing and wages and benefits.

Narayana Murthy, the founder of Infosys Technologies, one of India's biggest IT company said, 'I was convinced that you can't solve poverty by "isms", but by first creating wealth through legal and ethical means, and then distributing it.'

Evil is termed as sin because it has the power to attract the mind. It acts upon our mind and heart to do what nature desires, even when such acts are prohibited by the laws of society. We feel guilty doing things that nature has designed as perfectly natural. *Tao Te Ching* states:

> When people see some things as beautiful,
> other things become ugly.
> When people see some things as good,
> other things become evil.
>
> Being and non-being create each other.
> Difficult and easy support each other.
> Long and short define each other.
> High and low depend on each other.
> Before and after follow each other.

As evil is contained in every good, the greatest challenge before a leader is to conceal evil in the garb of goodness.

Most people want to see only goodness and therefore, follow people they view as good because their evils are not known to them.

A leader may have to choose evil for the good of his people. This is not easy as most people are scared of choosing evil over good—like no actor wants to play the role of a villain, even in a drama. Few leaders want to run the risk of being remembered as an evil person in case they fail in their goals. But if you prefer to choose only the good and righteous path, your chances of success are considerably reduced. You may fail to acquire the power and wealth necessary to empower your people and fulfil their needs.

A leader is one who chooses the interest of his followers over his personal ignominy. He can beg, steal and even snatch for the followers. He suffers individual loss for the sake of the gain of his followers. That makes him a leader whom people follow because they themselves do not have the courage to do so. People do not mind if someone else does all the dirty jobs for them while they can enjoy the fruits without getting their own hands dirty.

3

Balancing Love with Hatred

Nature is at work. Character and destiny are her handiwork. She gives us love and hate, jealousy and reverence. All that is ours is the power to choose which impulse we shall follow.

—David Seabury

Everyone seeks love and wants to be loved. Martin Luther King Jr said, 'I have decided to stick with love. Hate is too great a burden to bear.' Love is often equated with God and the deepest knowledge of the world. Hence, one who can sacrifice love for anything, makes the greatest sacrifice for the cause.

The path of a leader is often filled with hatred. In the long history of the world, there may be only a handful of leaders who were not hated, and the same is likely in future. Consider how John Francis 'Jack' Welch, the legendary chairman and CEO of General Electric, between 1981 and 2001 became a great leader in the corporate world.

Welch became GE's youngest chairman and CEO in 1981, succeeding Reginald H Jones. By 1982, Welch had dismantled much of the earlier management put together by Jones and led an aggressive simplification and consolidation initiative.

Welch worked to eradicate perceived inefficiency by trimming inventories and dismantling the bureaucracy. He closed factories, reduced payrolls and cut lacklustre old-line units. Each year, Welch would fire the bottom 10 per cent of his managers, irrespective of absolute performance. He earned a reputation for brutal candour in his meetings with executives. He rewarded those in the top 20 per cent with bonuses and stock options. He also expanded the broadness of the stock options program at GE from just top executives to nearly one-third of all employees. During the early 1980s he was dubbed 'Neutron Jack' (in reference to the neutron bomb) for eliminating employees while leaving buildings intact.

Welch received wide criticism for his lack of compassion for the middle class and the working class. He fired hundreds of workers from his company and kept the rest under constant pressure and threat. Still he was considered a great leader, as under him GE became one of the top corporates in the world—during his tenure, the company's value rose by 4000 per cent.

We praise our leaders when they act against our adversaries. But when our own interest is threatened, we begin to dislike the same leaders, irrespective of the sincerity of their intentions. An effective leader is bound to create enemies. British leader, Winston Churchill rightly said, 'You have enemies? Good. That means you've stood up for something, sometime in your life.'

The same leaders are also loved by people who benefitted from their actions. They are loved even after their die. People still recall Lincoln, Churchill and Gandhi with much love and respect, even though millions hated them in their lifetime.

Hatred is the emotional price leaders must pay for getting love and honour.

The Power of Hatred

What drives a man to be a leader? Is it love? Is it hatred?

Love often leads to bonding and prevents a person from taking a dangerous path. When Chanakya was humiliated by the Nanda king in Magadha, he was filled with hatred for that dynasty. Chanakya took an oath to eradicate the Nanda empire, and not to tie his hair till he fulfilled his oath. He ultimately plotted to defeat Nandas with the help of Chandragupta.

> Chanakya entered the palace of the Nandas. He saw ten gold plates and thrones. He was told that nine were for the eight Nanda princes, and their father, Sarvarthasiddhi. The tenth was for the most learned person in Vedas. It was occupied by Subandhu, whose incompetence was widely known. Chanakya sat down on the tenth throne. The nine princes and Subandhu entered the place and noticed Chanakya sitting on the throne. The youngest two brothers, Sukalpa and Dhanananda, asked him to get up and leave. Chanakya replied, 'I am the most qualified for the tenth throne. It is my right to sit on it. If Subandhu defeats me in a literary debate, I will readily step down.'
>
> The princes became angry, but Chanakya remained calm and continued his request for a debate. Sukalpa insulted him by calling him a monkey, but Chanakya continued to be calm and said that the duty of the king is to obey the dharma. Since the tenth throne is to be given to the most learned man, it is *dharmic* that a contest must be held. Further, Chanakya also pointed out that he may be black like a monkey, but scholars are noted for what is within them.
>
> The princes got angry and asked the guards to throw him out

by pulling him by the tuft of his hair. It was then that Chanakya took his famous oath, 'I will not tie my tuft of hair until I uproot the whole Nanda dynasty and establish dharma in Magadha. Rulers like you have spoiled Bharat–India. The tuft of hair, which you arrogantly pull now will be like a serpent which comes back to bite you.'

When Gandhi was thrown out of the first class compartment in South Africa in the winter chill, he decided to fight against the racist powers. His fight culminated with the British finally leaving India after almost half a century.

Hatred is very powerful. It can overpower love. When a man burns in the fire of hatred, he cannot feel any love, and is willing to destroy his enemy even if it kills him. It is amazing to note that a leader who may be driven to act against another in hatred, may be showered with love in the process. People who share his hatred may love him for rising up to the challenge.

Buddha, who taught only love and compassion, too was driven by his hatred for the life of luxury, power and recreation. While Jesus Christ was full of love, yet his abhorrence for the ruthless system of Judaism may have contained an element of hatred. Christ had cried out:

> Woe to you, scribes and Pharisees, hypocrites! for you tithe mint and dill and cummin, and have neglected the weightier matters of the law, justice and mercy and faith; these you ought to have done, without neglecting the others. You blind guides, straining out a gnat and swallowing a camel!... Woe to you, scribes and Pharisees, hypocrites! For you are like whitewashed tombs, which outwardly appear beautiful, but within they are full of dead men's bones and all uncleanness.
>
> You snakes! You brood of vipers! How will you escape being condemned to hell? (Matthew 23)

As the world gives back to us what we give to it, hatred surely invites hatred. Buddha's family disliked him for abandoning them and his duties as a householder. Even after he became enlightened, when people left their families to follow Buddha and became monks, their families did not forgive Buddha. Jesus incurred the hatred of not only the priests, but also the common man who celebrated when he was crucified.

A leader cannot avoid being hated. This hatred is directly proportional to his influence and power. A person who does not wish to be hated should avoid leadership roles.

Hatred is the price that society extracts from its leaders for the honour, power and wealth it bestows unto them.

Power Breeds Hatred

A rich man is hated by the poor for being rich and a powerful man is hated by those who wield no authority. A leader is a combination of both and hence, hatred for him is manifold. If a powerful person like a king gives up his power and empowers everyone, then also he may invite hatred for having become powerless.

Even when a person acquires wealth by legal and ethical means, he may be hated by those who are jealous of his success. It is human nature to find fault in others who succeed than to find fault in the self—because when you find fault within, you have to overcome your fault, which most people don't want to do. Finding fault in others makes it easy to criticise them and overlook the need for self-improvement. Hence, most people hate successful people for their small little faults rather than appreciating them for their great strengths.

A leader is criticised for whatever he does as all his actions benefit some and adversely affect others. When other people commit the same mistake, they can be forgiven or ignored, but never a leader, for his actions affect a large number of people. Even if it is a win-win proposition, some people will gain more than others, and the ones who gain less become inimical to the leader. This is because people focus more on their notional disadvantage than the advantage.

A leader is obliged to fulfil his mission and meet the expectations of his followers. But no leader can deliver all by himself, so he delegates work to others. To meet his high targets, he must pressurise his subordinates to deliver. He may often lose his temper when he sees inefficiency, and when harsh words are uttered, the hatred for the leaders is fanned.

No Leader Can Avoid the Media

Leaders rely a lot on the media to become popular and connect with their followers. However, once the leaders become popular, the media needs their support to increase their TRPs. Fall of a hero is good for media ratings, which is more interested in stories that highlight human weaknesses than the strength of people. The media attacks leaders more than common people as this is likely to please the maximum number of people.

Social media can be a dangerous tool to malign a leader. One is likely to find more ridicule, defamation and maligning on social media than appreciation. Any person will be hurt when he is criticised in public. We enjoy criticism only if it is against others. When you read your own criticism in the media, you are likely to be filled with anger and hatred.

Yet, a wise leader knows that nothing is free in this world. Fame has to come with ignominy and love with hatred. One must focus on positive things to shun the negativity.

Love: The Antidote of Hatred

A leader focuses on the good things done by him, ignoring the negatives said about him. It would be foolish to measure a leader by the hatred he generates because great leaders are both hated and loved by a large number of people. A leader must evoke much love from his deeds, as that is the only antidote to counter all hatred and make good progress.

1. **Love Yourself:** Great leaders have a great sense of self-worth. They know in their hearts what good work they are doing. If you stand well in your own eyes, you can withstand any amount of criticism.
2. **Love Your People:** Good leaders have much love for their followers, which far overweighs any hatred they may have for their enemies. In time, leaders learn to take any criticism by their opponents positively and view it as a mark of achievement.
3. **Love Your Job:** Leaders must love their job. They have to understand that in order to clean the house, you have to get dirty. It is easy to sit outside and laugh at those doing the dirty work. But it requires much wisdom to imagine what will happen if people do not clean the dirt and filth.

Making a Choice—Love or Hatred?

To choose between love and hatred is the greatest dilemma of a leader. Who wants hatred? Just like no one wants to be sick and everyone wishes to be healthy, no one wishes to be hated. Yet, wise men know that there are no free lunches in the world.

Leaders must pay heed to all criticism and try to address them as much as they can. They also need to avoid acts that invite criticism without giving them adequate benefit. In the end, however, they must learn to live with hatred and criticism.

Love and hatred come in a package. Your desire to be loved must be balanced with your ability to withstand hatred. If you are too sensitive to criticism, then you must shun appreciation also. Instead of seeking appreciation, focus on your work and let the work speak for itself. Distribute the credit for the work among all team members, and the criticism shall also get proportionally reduced.

4

Dealing with Both the Lower and the Higher Self

Spiritual relationship is far more precious than physical. Physical relationship divorced from spiritual is body without soul.

–Mahatma Gandhi

Man is the most evolved animal in this world. We started our journey like any other animal, yet we evolved due to the presence of divine spirit within us, which pulls us continuously towards our spiritual self. Pierre Teilhard de Chardin, a French Jesuit priest and a philosopher said, 'We are not human beings on a spiritual journey. We are spiritual beings on a human journey.' In India, an age-old belief is that we are all striving for divinity and when we achieve divinity, we become free from the cycle of birth and death.

Every person in this world has a dual nature that reflects both the beast and the divine within. Animal instincts like hunger, passion, sex etc. coexist with an inherent desire to imbibe divine traits like love, compassion and sense of justice. We can call the former our 'lower self', while the latter denotes our 'higher self'.

The Lower Self

Since man evolved from an animal, he cannot let go of many of his beastly attributes. We generally act selfish and care not much about others. All that interests us is usually our own welfare and that of our family and relatives. It is rare to find someone treating the entire humanity like his family. We find that people don't mind telling lies, pulling down others or bending rules to derive benefits from others. Here is a fine example:

> A lawyer and an engineer were fishing in the Caribbean when they got talking. The lawyer mentioned, 'I'm here because my house burned down and everything got destroyed by the fire. The insurance company paid for everything.'
>
> 'That's quite a coincidence,' remarked the engineer. 'I'm here because my house and all my belongings were destroyed by a flood. My insurance company too paid for everything.'
>
> There was a brief pause, and then the puzzled lawyer asked, 'How do you start a flood?'

Any pragmatic leader cannot ignore the lower desires of his people. People want money, power and position in the society whether they deserve it or not. They are also not concerned about the character of the leader so far as the leader is able to give them what they want. This is true not only in the political arena, but also in the corporate world. As long as the shareholders are getting good returns on their investments, they are least interested in what the company does. In fact, investors readily ditch a company even if it is known to follow the best practices and highest ethical standards, but offers poor return on investments.

India being a developing economy, many successful leaders in politics and corporates are not known to be ethical. People too vote the corrupt and criminal to power again and again, ignoring leaders known to be ethical because only the corrupt can help the corrupt. During election time, it is common to see politicians distributing money and alcohol to the voters to garner votes. But once the election is over, the same politician extracts money from the same people for doing any job for them.

> Four guys went for golfing; one went into the clubhouse to pay, while others waited at the first tee.
>
> One of the guys says, 'I'm so proud of my son. He is a stock broker and he's made enough, so much that he just gave away a huge portfolio.'
>
> The next guy said, 'I'm so proud of my son. He's a car dealer and is doing so well, he just gave away a Ferrari.'
>
> The third guy says, 'I'm so proud of my son. He's got enough money. In fact, he just gave away a million-dollar home.'
>
> Just as the third guy finishes talking, the fourth guy joins them and asks, 'What are you guys talking about?'
>
> 'Just about how good our sons are doing,' the three men replied in a chorus.
>
> 'Well, my son is doing very well too,' says the fourth man. 'He's a politician, and just last week, he got a huge portfolio, a Ferrari and a million-dollar home.'

Leaders are usually a reflection of the people they lead. How can a leader be moral if his people are immoral? Voltaire has rightly said, 'The public is a ferocious beast; one must either chain it or flee from it.' Only a more savage beast can control the beasts of the society. Even robbers need a leader to succeed in their mission.

Leadership can be quite difficult because often you have no option but to follow the ethics and values of the people you lead. You must understand that 'the followers are as they are', and not 'what they should be'. You must know their expectation and be willing to fulfil them. In the test of leadership, the winner constantly competes with others who are willing to give greater satisfaction to their followers.

Napoleon has rightly said, 'A leader is a dealer on hope.' You can win people over for a short time by giving them hope, but the same people would curse and even kill you, if you fail to fulfil their hopes.

> On a Friday afternoon, a young man walked into a jewellery shop with a beautiful young woman.
>
> The girl selected a magnificent necklace.
>
> The man said to the jeweller, 'We are going out of town for the weekend and will be back to pick it up on Monday.'
>
> The couple left the store.
>
> On Monday, the young man came to the shop and said to the jeweller, 'I did not want to purchase that necklace. I have come to sincerely thank you for helping me have a really wonderful weekend.'

Offering hope to someone is not less than a commitment. There are leaders who make exceptional promises with no intentions of fulfilling them and often beat the genuine leader in the game. But they later face wide condemnation by the people. Leadership is not a job where you contribute what you can. It is a total commitment.

> A chicken and a pig decided to go into town and look for a job in the city. They spotted a sign in a restaurant window that read: 'Ham and eggs: $1.50.'
>
> The chicken suggested they go in, but the pig refused.
>
> He said to the chicken, 'For you, going in is just a contribution; for me, it's a total commitment.'

The Higher Self

While it is easy to see that people are selfish and solely interested in fulfilling their personal desires, it is also a fact that we all aspire to become better human beings and hence, we also want our leaders to be better than us. You do not wish to be taught by a teacher who knows less than you. Even the corrupt thus expect honesty from their leader and an honest leader induces people to be honest not only by inspiration but also through fear of punishment. Take the case of this honest man, whose conscience was so powerful that he decided to pay his taxes honestly to the Tax Department.

> A man sent a letter to the Income Tax Department saying, 'Enclosed is a cheque for $1,000. I cheated on my taxes last year and I can't sleep at night.
>
> PS: If I still can't sleep, I'll send you the rest I owe you.'

Followers are very clever. They wish to share their leader's fortune, but not their sins. Even voters who voted for corrupt politicians are quick to curse them when these leaders get caught for bribery or other illegal acts. Most people seek honesty, integrity and character from their leaders. The more corrupt an organisation or a nation is, the greater is the demand of integrity from its leaders.

The reason for this dichotomy is the conflict that always exists in the mind of the individual and the society. We wish to be divine, but we do not wish to sacrifice personal benefits. While it takes years for a good habit to produce results, the base habits fulfil our desires instantly. Hence, there are leaders in every nation who are able to appeal to the higher self of the population and garner their support by following legal and ethical practices. Their numbers may be few, but their following is large and lasting because that is what people want to be. It is these leaders who transform the society and the people with the power of their soul, by following the path of righteousness.

Balancing the Lower and Higher Self

In every field, a leader must balance between the lower and the higher self of his people, both at an individual level and a social level. A successful leader attracts not only people who really follow his principles, but also those who actually exploit leaders for their own purpose.

> A man went to the confession box and told the priest, 'Bless me father, for I have sinned. I have been with a loose woman.'
>
> 'Who were you with?'
>
> 'I would rather not say that father.'
>
> 'Was it Alisha?'
>
> 'No, Father.'
>
> 'Was it Zara?'
>
> 'No, Father.'
>
> 'Was it Julie?'
>
> 'No, Father.'
>
> 'Well. Pray God for mercy. Pray God. He shall forgive your sin.'
>
> When the man came out, his friend asked, 'How was it?'
>
> 'It was fantastic. I got forgiveness for my sin and also three leads to pursue.'

If more people are successful invoking the lower self of the people, it is because they are themselves at the lower level. To attract the higher self, your own self must grow. Once a person of higher self appears on the stage, all leaders with lower selves start looking like pygmies. This is what happened when Gandhi emerged on the scene during India's freedom movement. His spirituality lifted the level of the struggle and gave rise to the best leaders India ever had. Peter Drucker has rightly said, 'In human affairs, the distance between the leaders and the average is a constant. If leadership performance is high, the average will go up.' A great leader lifts the moral standard of the whole society, while a mean leader causes it to decay.

Leaders have to learn to take care of both body and soul of the people, which represent respectively the lower and higher self. Balancing this lower and higher self is necessary for leaders, as well as for each one of us.

5

Balancing the Masculine with the Feminine

'The Pentacle—the ancients envisioned their world in two halves—masculine and feminine. Their gods and goddesses worked to keep a balance of power. Yin and Yang. When male and female were balanced, there was harmony in the world. When they were unbalanced, there was chaos.'

—Dan Brown, Da Vinci Code

In Chinese philosophy, the concept of yin-yang is used to describe how seemingly opposite or contrary forces are interconnected and interdependent in the natural world. They give rise to each other as they relate to one another like the positive and negative charges. The same womb of mother gives birth to both male and female children who are so different from each other. The masculine and feminine are always balanced by nature.

In the ancient Indian tradition, there is the concept of *Ardhanarishvara*, which is a composite androgynous form of the Hindu god Shiva and his consort Parvati. *Ardhanarishvara* represents the synthesis of masculine and feminine energies of the universe—Purusha and Prakriti, and illustrates how Shakti—the female principle of God, is inseparable from Shiva—the male principle of God.

The world has always been governed by both male and female. Even if the masculine is more visible, the feminine is no less important. The concept of Yin-Yang can be represented as following:

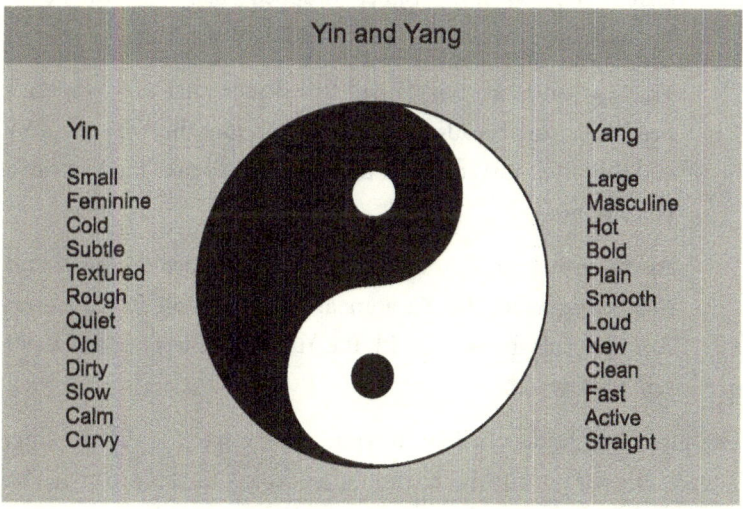

Since ages, there has been conflict and also attraction between the two. When one aspect rises in an individual or the society, there is discomfort and chaos, and soon the other aspect rises in proportion to balance the former.

We need balance of masculine and feminine energies for effective leadership. Masculine leaders are generally ruthless, bold and restless, producing quick results often by demolishing their opponents. Their style generates hatred and distrust. Such leaders are full of courage and not afraid of death.

> In February of 1519, a general by the name Hernando Cortez set sail on the final leg of an ocean voyage that was to take him

from Cuba to the distant shores of the Yucatan, Mexico. Cortez, who had heard of the great riches of the Yucatan and had set his mind on conquering them, was in charge of eleven ships with more than 500 soldiers, 100 sailors and 16 horses.

When Cortez and company finally arrived on shore, Cortez suddenly turned to his men and ordered them to 'Burn the boats!' The jaws of his soldiers dropped open. Burn the boats! Then, how in the world were they going to get back?

That's when Cortez explained to his men that they wouldn't need the boats because they would conquer the Yucatan army and gain their fortune. And then they would take the Yucatan's boats home!

As the story goes, Cortez and his men did burn the boats and then conquered the Yucatan army, taking all its treasures. And they left the island with the Yucatan's boats just as Cortez said they would.

The masculine leaders believe in winning by force in a direct battle. They would either kill the enemy or get killed in the process. The masculine method of leadership is quite effective, but also destructive. It suits leaders who are more powerful than their opponents.

On the other side, the feminine style of leadership is convincing, attractive and can make people do things 'which the leaders want them to do'. Non-violence, charm, love and compassion are the traits of a feminine leader. This style is slow in producing results for it employs non-violent means. Females generally tend to shun violence and can entice. Men are usually contrary to this. 'Globally, men committed 95 per cent of murders in 2012' as per the United Nations Office on Drugs and Crime (UNODC) reports of 2014.

Leaders who perfect the feminine style prefer to defeat the opponent by employing deceit, lies, charm, persuasion and causing rift within the opposing team, following policies like divide and rule. This style is suitable when you have less power or when you do not want to use force to decide the issue.

Why Leaders Strive to Strike a Balance

Leaders are often confused between the masculine and feminine methods of leadership. By following the former, they can produce results quickly. But in the process, they generate tremendous hatred. The latter method requires much humility, trust, intelligence and patience since the results are slow. A great leader balances the two aspects, using the force of a lion as well as the deceit of a fox, depending on the situation.

Deceit may be criticised by ethical people, but sometimes it is better to deceive, to avoid the destruction accompanying war and save the lives of men caught in battle. It is possible to win with minimum force if you can deceive tactfully. Hitler, Alexander and Napoleon were typically dominating masculine leaders, while Buddha, Gandhi, Nelson Mandela and Martin Luther King employed feminine qualities effectively.

Lincoln and Akbar can be called balanced leaders who used force, but without hatred and malice. The feminine traits become extremely important when you are battling your own people or the opponents are too strong. If the battle is fierce and full of hatred, you end up only with debris. So you lose even when you win. Abraham Lincoln's second inaugural address reveals his love for everyone, even during the Civil War:

> With malice towards none; with charity for all; with firmness in the right, as God gives us to see the right, let us strive on to finish the work we are in; to bind up the nation's wounds; to care for him who shall have borne the battle and for his widow and his orphan. To do all which may achieve and cherish a just and a lasting peace among ourselves and with the world.

A good leader accomplishes his mission with perfect balance. Napoleon Bonaparte said, 'I am sometimes a fox and sometimes a lion. The whole secret of government lies in knowing when to be the one or the other.'

6

Equality or Differentiation?

The society which scorns excellence in plumbing as a humble activity and tolerates shoddiness in philosophy because it is an exalted activity will have neither good plumbing nor good philosophy: Neither its pipes nor its theories will hold water.

—John W Gardner

'If a man is called to be a street sweeper, he should sweep streets even as a Michelangelo painted or Beethoven composed music or Shakespeare wrote poetry,' said Martin Luther King Jr. 'He should sweep streets so well that all the hosts of heaven and earth will pause to say, "Here lived a great street sweeper who did his job well."'

There is no other way to lift the society than to motivate everyone in the society to achieve excellence in their work. If everyone in a nation strives to excel, the nation would automatically become the greatest in the world. Yet, we see that most people fail to do that. As a result many nations remain poor and underdeveloped. The same is true with individuals.

Michael Jordan, who is regarded as the greatest basketball player of all time once said, 'To be successful you have to be selfish or else you never achieve. And once you get to your highest level, then you have to be unselfish. Stay reachable. Stay in touch. Don't isolate.'

There has been an eternal conflict between equality and differentiation. If everyone is treated equally, there is no incentive to work hard. People will be unwilling to sweat when rewards do not commensurate with effort.

People often advocate equality in the name of God or for the sake of humanity, which is not at all true. God made us all diverse and unique individuals. Some are more beautiful than others, some more intelligent or healthy than the rest, and so on. In fact, no two people in the world are alike or equal in absolute terms. Even siblings are often poles apart.

Treating everyone equal is the surest recipe for disaster. Jack Welch, the legendary CEO of General Electric does not mince words when he says,

> Companies win when their managers make a clear and meaningful distinction between top and bottom-performing businesses and people, when they cultivate the strong and cull the weak. Companies suffer when every business and person is treated equally and bets are sprinkled all around like rain on the ocean.... If that sounds Darwinian, let me add that I am convinced that along with being the most efficient and most effective way to run your company, differentiation also happens to be the fairest and kindest. Ultimately, it makes a winner out of everyone.

Let us imagine that you are working in an organisation where everyone is paid the same salary and facilities are uniform. The promotion is based purely on seniority and there is a small growth of salary upon promotion. There is no distinction between people who are working long hours and those who sit idle. There is no appreciation of honesty and no punishment for corruption. In short, everyone is treated equal in the organisation.

It is almost impossible for such an organisation to achieve excellence as it can never create excellent individuals. Yet, the organisation can be rated very high on the scale of equality.

But is it fair to treat everyone equal and give no importance to their contribution in the organisation?

Now let us imagine another society where age, qualification, sex, race etc. are of no consequence and the only determinant attribute is performance. People are promoted and paid purely on the basis of their contribution to the company. If you help the company profit, you benefit in proportion.

There is no doubt that such an organisation would produce excellent individuals who would become role models for others. Everyone shall strive to give their best and the entire organisation shall benefit.

However, such an organisation or country shall be rated very poorly on the scale of equality as the top performer's income and privileges may be hundredfold higher than that of the one who performs the worst. The one on the top might feel his higher income is justified, but the one at the bottom may term it unjust.

The Power of Excellence

While treating everyone equal is a sure recipe for mediocrity, treating differentially is not a sure way for excellence unless the differentiation is fair, just and transparent. Just like a leader can create a large number of leaders, an excellent performer can create many excellent performers. It is part of human nature to grow and become better when we have role models and higher benchmarks. In order to improve the self, men look up to people who have fared better. Leaders may create jealousy and envy in some, but they also foster the spirit of competition and desire to excel in many.

Lord Krishna says, 'Whatever action a great man performs, common men follow. And whatever standards he sets by exemplary acts, all the world pursues.'

What great leaders do, people follow.

The excellence of an organisation can be measured by the excellent people it produces. If excellence is respected and rewarded, everyone gives his best and the country becomes great. No country can become great if it does not have great individuals. As the American author, John W Gardner said, 'Excellence is doing ordinary things extraordinarily well.' When even ordinary people choose to excel in their work, who can stop a nation from becoming the best?

The Crab Mentality

While the drive to excel makes a country great, it also creates inequality between men. Since only few can rise to the top, those at the bottom lose incentive and try to pull down the excellent people to their own level. This is termed as 'crab mentality', best described by the phrase, 'If I can't have it, neither can you.' The metaphor refers to a pot of crabs. Individually the crabs could easily escape from the pot, but instead, they grab at each other in a useless 'king of the hill' competition which prevents any from escaping and ensures their collective demise. People sometimes relish less what they get as compared to what others lose, as is evident from this fable.

> Two neighbours came before Jupiter and entreated him to grant their hearts' desire. Now, one was full of avarice and the other eaten up with envy. So to punish them both, Jupiter granted that each might have whatever he wished for himself, but only on the condition that his neighbour had twice as much.

The avaricious man prayed to have a room full of gold. No sooner had he said that, it was done, but all his joy was turned to grief when he found that his neighbour had two rooms full of the precious metal.

Then came the turn of the envious man, who could not bear to know that his neighbour had any joy at all. So he prayed that he might have one of his own eyes put out, which would ensure his companion would become totally blind.

There always seem to be more people who have no desire to become excellent or feel sure they cannot excel, so their job is to pull down anyone who tries to achieve excellence.

Making a Choice

It is never easy for any leader to choose between differentiation and equality. You are condemned either way. When you treat everyone equally, you are considered just by majority as equality benefits below-average people and they seem to always be in majority. At the same time, you are also condemned because you can't produce results with people having a crab mentality. However, if you choose to reward the excellent and punish the non-performer, you achieve the desired results but get condemned for being unfair, unjust, cruel and Darwinian.

In any country, almost 90 per cent of the wealth and power is concentrated in the hands of less than 10 per cent of the people. Hence, the bottom 90 per cent is always envious of the top 10 per cent and would love to pull them down or see their wealth and power evenly distributed. If they want to rise, they have to work hard, but it is easier to simply pull down achievers, making the rich less rich and powerful less powerful. Hence, the appeal of equality in the name of justice has always been very popular. In a democracy, where numbers are the key for deciding right and wrong, it becomes difficult to ignore public opinion.

If the leader chooses equality, he can make more people happy, but the same people would criticise him later for failing to produce results. Once people with excellence stop performing their best, everyone falls below their potential and eventually, everyone loses. The poor would get poorer even if the rich become less rich. The poor would suffer much more due to the scarcity of resources than the rich, who might still have enough to live a comfortable life.

A leader has to balance the two aspects and must be willing to face criticism, which awaits him either way. If his vision is long-term and he really cares for the people and the organisation, he has no option but to follow differentiation. However, if his goal is selfish and his vision is short-term, nothing sells like the cry of equality and justice. He can't afford to follow one path exclusively because he has to balance the hearts and heads of the people. Equality appeals more to the heart, while the head always points towards differentiation.

PART III

THE NECESSARY EVILS OF LEADERS

1

A Burning Desire to Lead and Achieve

To burn with desire and keep quiet about it is the greatest punishment we can bring on ourselves.

—Federico Garcia Lorca

Desire is considered to be the main cause of all suffering. Lord Krishna teaches in Gita, 'In a man brooding on the object of senses, attachment to them springs up; attachment begets desire and desire brings wrath. Wrath breeds confusion which leads to loss of memory which ruins reason which spells the destruction of man.'

Gautama Buddha also presented Four Noble Truths to the world:

1. Life is suffering
2. All suffering is caused by desire
3. All desires must be extinguished by the person who wishes freedom from suffering
4. Follow eight-fold path for the cessation of suffering

Yet, it is desire and ambition that is the source of all leadership qualities, which enables a leader to achieve great things in life. American writer Harry A Overstreet in his book *Influencing Human Behavior*, said:

> Action springs out of what we fundamentally desire...and the best piece of advice which can be given to would-be persuaders, whether in business, in the home, in the school, in politics is: First, arouse in the other person an eager want. He who can do this has the whole world with him. He who can't, walks a lonely way.

Only when we have a burning desire to achieve something in life, can we sacrifice the small things in life that give us instant joy and happiness, and work for something which may give us joy in future, even if it gives pain now. Gita describes different types of pleasures for men as:

1. **Sattvik Pleasure:** Which is gained by repeated practice and which puts an end to the pain. Which at inception looks like poison but in the end is like nectar, born of serene realisation of the true nature of Self–Atman. (Gita 18: 36-37)
2. **Rajsik Pleasure:** Which arising from the contact of the senses with their objects, is first as nectar, but in the end like poison. (Gita 18: 38)
3. **Tamsik Pleasure:** Which arises from sleep and sloth and senseless action; which corrupts the conscience, both in the beginning and in the end. (Gita 18:39)

You must have wisdom to enjoy the *sattvik* pleasures of life. You must have wealth and power to enjoy the *rajsik* pleasure. If you have neither wisdom nor wealth or power, you can enjoy the tamsik pleasure by criticising everyone and doing nothing. Here's a fine example of *tamsik* pleasure:

> Wife complained to her husband, 'We should be absolutely ashamed of the way we live. Mother pays our rent. My aunt buys

our clothes. My sister sends us money for food. We should be ashamed that we can't do better than that.'

The husband replied, 'Why should we be ashamed? What about your two uncles who are not sending us anything at all. They should be ashamed.'

Leaders are made because of their burning desire for *rajsik* pleasure—a passion for wealth or power or both. You cannot become a leader if you desire only wisdom or have no desires. Desire is the fuel that propels leaders towards success. That is why often *rajsik* nature is associated with the nature of kings—rajas.

We may have great desires as a child and at that point, believe we can do anything and everything. Yet, as we grow older, we change. As popular author, Paulo Coelho writes in *The Alchemist*:

> We are told from childhood onward that everything we want to do is impossible. We grow up with this idea, and as the years accumulate, so too do the layers of prejudice, fear and guilt. There comes a time when our personal calling is so deeply buried in our soul as to be invisible. But it's still there.

While most people bury their desires to gain peace in life, leaders reignite their deep-seated desires. And it is on the path of fulfilling these desires that a person displays much courage, passion, vision and strong imagination—traits that define him as a leader. You may read thousands of books and attend hundreds of leadership seminars, but in the absence of a compelling desire to win in life, you're unlikely to rise.

Wealth is the foundation to a comfortable life for it fulfils much of your physical needs and even future spiritual needs. If you are not sure of your next meal, there is little chance of reaching any higher level. There is nothing wrong in accumulating wealth, since only when you have wealth, you can give wealth to others and solve their basic problems.

Wealth is a must for physical and sensual pleasures, as much as to help others. Business, industry leaders and top managers have great desire for wealth, which drives them to work hard and succeed.

In order to change the world, you also need power. You cannot generally exercise your free will in the absence of power. If you have no authority, you may find it difficult to express and actualise your stand in life. Even to help others, protect your loved ones and live a life of dignity, one needs power. When you see injustice, inequality and poverty in this world, you are likely to feel disturbed and would wish to change things for the better—hence, you desire power. All leaders crave power so that they can change the world.

It is not easy to forgo the instant pleasures of life for the sake of benefits that may accrue tomorrow. Only when people develop a burning desire for anything can they sacrifice the comforts of today to make a better tomorrow. When a desire is deep, it reaches the subconscious mind and calls for cultivation of qualities that will help fulfil such desires, and this is what transforms an ordinary person into a great leader.

There is no limit to desires. As the poet Ghalib said, 'I have thousands of desires, each worth dying for. Many of them I have realised, yet I yearn for more.' The problem is that desires keep changing with time. When one desire is fulfilled, another is born and once that is fulfilled, yet another takes shape. This is why many people can't lead, as they do not know where to go or which desire to fulfil. In writer Lewis Carroll's *Alice in Wonderland*, the following conversation between Alice and the Cheshire Cat is quite interesting:

> 'Would you tell me, please, which way I ought to go from here?'
>
> 'That depends a good deal on where you want to get to,' said the Cat.
>
> 'I don't much care where....' said Alice.
>
> 'Then it doesn't matter which way you go,' said the Cat.

> '...so long as I get SOMEWHERE,' Alice added as an explanation.
>
> 'Oh, you're sure to do that,' said the Cat, 'if you only walk long enough.'

Lewis Carroll has rightly said, 'If you don't know where you're going, any road will get you there.' It is because every road takes a person 'somewhere' and a person, who does not know where to go, would surely reach 'somewhere'. That is what most people do. They just live their life to get 'something', be 'somebody' and reach 'somewhere'.

A leader must concentrate his mind and focus on one desire only. You can't have everything in your life. For example, at times it may be difficult for leaders to have both wealth as well as power in abundance. The salary of the US president, the most powerful person in the world, is merely US $400,000 per year, which is less than the wealth Bill Gates—the richest man in the world, creates in a day. Yet, Bill Gates wields no real power. Unlike the US president, he cannot bring about any policy changes or influence national and international events.

You have to sacrifice something to gain anything. Leaders have to sacrifice many of their desires and focus all their energy on a single desire only. For example, Abraham Lincoln is remembered as one of the greatest presidents of the United States for his single-minded pursuit of one goal: Freedom of the slaves. Anecdotes from Lincoln's life reveal his burning and singular passion.

> Judge T Lyle Dickey of Illinois related that when the excitement over the Kansas-Nebraska Bill first broke out, he was with Lincoln and several friends attending court. One evening, several people, including he and Lincoln, were discussing the slavery question.
>
> Judge Dickey contended that slavery was an institution that the Constitution recognised, and which could not be disturbed. Lincoln argued that ultimately slavery must become extinct.

'After a while,' said Judge Dickey, 'we went upstairs to bed. There were two beds in our room, and I remember that Lincoln sat up in his nightshirt, on the edge of the bed, arguing the point with me. At last we went off to sleep.

Early in the morning I woke up and there was Lincoln, half sitting up in bed. 'Dickey,' said he, 'I tell you this nation cannot exist half slave and half free.'

'Oh, Lincoln,' said I, 'go to sleep.'

When we try to have 'something of everything', we end up being ordinary and common. Only when you decide to have 'everything of something', so much that you are willing to sacrifice everything for that one desire, you succeed as a leader—like a lens that focuses all the sunlight at one point on the paper to burn it. That is the burning desire.

2

The Hunger for Power

To know the pains of power, we must go to those who have it; to know its pleasures, we must go to those who are seeking it: The pains of power are real, its pleasures imaginary.

—Charles Caleb Colton, Lacon

Leaders must perform, and no performance is possible without power. In physics, power is defined as the work delivered per unit time. The more powerful you are, the more work you can perform in unit time. The work itself is a product of force and displacement. For getting any work done, you require force and this force should be strong enough to move an object from one place to another. If there is no change in position, all the force is useless.

Force is integral to power as without force no work can be done. You may have all the knowledge, intelligence, plan and charm, but if you fail to perform, you are not a leader.

Most of us are fascinated by power. We refer to God as omnipotent meaning that He is all-powerful and can do anything. There is nothing beyond God. Perhaps because it is commonly believed that we too are a part of God, that we all harbour a secret desire to become all-powerful. Just like God is infinite, there is no limit to power. The more we have, the more we seek. Often, we even want to control the mind and soul of others.

We worship people who are powerful for we fear they may use that power against us. James Bond and Superman movies are a hit all over the world as these heroes can do anything. They can defeat entire armies of villains single-handedly. You are unlikely to ever see a meek and powerless person cast as a hero, simply because we don't want to be such a person.

Movies often create an impression that power and goodness are interrelated. They try to convince us that we too can control all crimes and bring goodness into the world simply by the brute use of power. Hence, the heroes are depicted as tall, muscular and handsome men because they must have a powerful body. In reality, the most powerful men in history like Alexander, Napoleon, Hitler, Stalin or Mao were all short and physically not very strong like superheroes. They also did not fight for goodness but mainly to fulfil their own ambitions. They were loved by few, but feared and hated by many.

Power Creates Hatred

Power is most detested in this world as we do not want to be subjected to it and thereby forced to do things that are not in accordance with our free will but according to the will of the people in power. While people want to use power against others, they hate it when power is used against them. Yet, a powerful person is often so intoxicated with power that he cannot feel the hatred of the people or understand their feelings. The intoxication of power is sometimes so potent that even saints turn into sinners under its influence. How the mighty often wear the crown of the greatest sinner, before whom every other sinner has to bow his head is told in this story.

Diomedes was a notorious pirate who had finally been captured and brought before the emperor for sentencing. Because of the pirate's many criminal deeds, everyone expected that Alexander would sentence the pirate to death. Before he passed judgment, however, Alexander decided to interview the pirate.

'What could possibly give you the right to sail the seas, taking by force things that do not belong to you?' Alexander asked the pirate.

Diomedes boldly replied with some questions of his own. 'O emperor,' he said, 'what could possibly give you the right to travel the whole world, taking by force things that do not belong to you? What gave you the right to occupy the land of Egypt? Who made you king of Persia? By what authority did you invade the land of India?'

Alexander stared at the man in amazement, and Diomedes went on speaking. 'Because I only use my own boat,' he said, 'I am called a pirate. You, however, use your army and your navy, and so you are proclaimed an emperor. If you ask me who the greater criminal is, I can't say. I do know, however, that if I had such weapons at my disposal, I would be an emperor too.'

Alexander was so impressed by this reply that instead of punishing the pirate, he let him go, praising him for his boldness and insight.

Power always creates hatred. Even if you use power objectively, you cannot escape making enemies when you use that power against someone. Thus, a wise person who seeks inner happiness desists from power. Author David Brin rightly said, 'It is said that power corrupts, but actually it's truer that power attracts the corruptible. The sane are usually attracted by other things than power.' That is why the dream of Plato to attract philosophers to be kings remained only utopian because a philosopher usually craves peace of mind more than power.

Leo Tolstoy, the Russian storyteller and great thinker also remarked, 'In order to obtain and hold power, a man must love it.' You'll find that we usually seek power to help ourselves and those whom we love. Another way of getting our work done is to employ charm and persuasion, but that is slow and also hurts our ego. How many of us like to request and beg others for work? Even if the work is done, our ego is crushed.

The Game of Power

Power games defy explanation. It is difficult to pinpoint the connect between a powerful man and the power he wields. What binds millions to a great leader so well that they become a force to reckon with, is a big mystery. Power is a reality which you cannot actually see or measure with an instrument. Power is acquired gradually. Just like a person does not grow rich overnight and a sportsman has to defeat many competitors in a series of games to win the championship crown, a man becomes powerful only after a prolonged battle, where he must overcome his rivals, one by one.

Only one who is infinitely powerful like God can perhaps defeat anyone and everyone in this world. In reality, no human being has been endowed with so much strength that he can defeat others easily. Even powerful leaders like Lincoln and John F Kennedy, former US presidents were felled by a single bullet.

It is the fear of failures, hatred and death, which keeps most people away from power. However, those who are desirous of being leaders must acquire power to defeat their enemies.

The acquisition of power by itself is immoral, even if it may be legal. When God has made everyone equal and all of us are the children of God, why should some people have the right to rule over others? A powerful person tries to change the world of God through force and will.

Yet, no society can last unless it is headed by a powerful leader. Most people would like to live life on their own terms and conditions and for their selfish interest. You need to exert power to make them work for the society and the country. Power is a necessary evil for all leaders.

3

Creating Fear

'Men go to far greater lengths to avoid what they fear than to obtain what they desire.'

—Dan Brown, The Da Vinci Code

Fear is an essential part of life. The fear of punishment keeps most people on track. Fear is important for the survival of the society as well as the individual. If people do not have fear of law or God, society would be in chaos. No one would then live peacefully at home or outside. There is no country where people follow the law voluntarily. Only if penalties are severe and implementation is ruthless do people fall in line. A nation where people do not fear their rulers, crumbles down like a house of cards.

> One day King Akbar said to his minister, Birbal, 'Birbal, my people are very obedient to me. They love me very much.' Birbal smiled and replied, 'This is true, but they fear you too.'
>
> Akbar could not agree to this, so it was decided that Birbal's statement should be tested.

Next day, according to Birbal's instructions, the king announced that he would be going hunting and people should pour a pot of milk in a tub kept in the courtyard. Next day when Akbar returned from his hunt, he found that there was no milk in the tub, instead there was only water. Akbar was very disappointed, but couldn't do anything.

Then Birbal said, 'This time you announce that you will come back and see the tub yourself.' The king did as Birbal said. Once again the tub was kept in the courtyard. This time when the king returned from the hunt, he found the tub overflowing with milk. Birbal said, 'I told you. It is your fear that made people obey you. The first time there was no one to check the tub, so people poured in water, but the second time, they knew you would check yourself, which is why they brought the milk.'

How Love Relates to Fear

No organisation can survive if there is no fear in the minds of the employees. While love is important and desirable, it is not the opposite of fear, rather it emanates from fear. More people fear God than love Him. Even those who love God, fear Him. In a family, the fear of losing each other's love and affection often binds the members. If they take each other for granted, love may dissipate.

The test of power is fear. God is feared because He is omnipotent. As long as people believe that God is omnipotent, they will fear Him and follow His commandments. Bible creates this fear in the minds of the people in the following words:

> When the Son of Man comes in His glory, all the nations will be gathered before Him, and He will separate people one from another as a shepherd separates his sheep from the goats, and He will set the sheep on His right hand but the goats at the left. Then He will also say to those on the left hand—'Depart from Me, you cursed, into the everlasting fire prepared for the devil

and his angels; for I was hungry and you gave Me no food, I was thirsty and you gave Me no drink, I was a stranger and you did not take Me in, naked and you did not clothe Me, sick and in prison and you did not visit Me.' ...'Assuredly, I say to you, inasmuch as you did not do it to one of the least of these, you did not do it to me.' And these will go away into everlasting punishment, but the righteous into eternal life.

Fear Is Essential to Rule

Only when a leader is feared and respected can he rule. The fear of a powerful leader should be felt not only outside but also within the organisation. It is only fear that stops people from questioning the decisions of their leader. When the leader is weak, everyone questions his decisions and seeks an explanation. The more he explains, the weaker the leader becomes. In the words of Chanakya, 'The power of a king lies in his mighty arms; that of a brahmin in his spiritual knowledge, and that of a woman in her beauty, youth and sweet words.'

However noble your goal may be, it is impossible to achieve it unless you severely punish those who obstruct your way. In a game of power, you have to create fear in the hearts and minds of all opponents.

Just like a lion rules the jungle through the fear he creates in the mind of other animals, a leader rules over his opponents and also his team. It is important to understand that there are many competitors and opponents of a leader who would like to occupy his place, even within his own organisation. A leader has to fear as much from his allies as from his enemies. Only fear counters fear. Machiavelli advises in his book *The Prince*,

> And here comes in the question whether it is better to be loved rather than feared, or feared rather than loved. It might perhaps be answered that we should wish to be both; but since love and

fear can hardly exist together, if we must choose between them, it is far safer to be feared than loved.

Whenever you wish to do anything in life, there is always an opposition. The level of opposition depends on the number of people who think they are more powerful than you. It is human nature that we all fear defeat. However, it is rare that we actually fight to prove our power, to learn if we will win or lose. Most battles are fought only in the mind. If you are really powerful, people will not dare oppose you. Once all opposition vanishes, you win all your battles without a fight.

> There was a terrible poisonous snake in a meadow. Everyone feared the snake. One day a saint was going along the meadow. The children playing there warned the saint of the snake and requested him not to go there. The saint however went ahead and soon he saw the snake with the hood. The saint recited a mantra, and the snake lay at his feet like an earthworm. The saint then advised the snake to pray to God, never to bite anyone and follow non-violence. The snake followed the advice and soon stopped hissing and biting anyone.
>
> Soon the boys noticed the change and started throwing stones on him. The snake got severely injured, but still did not react to the boys. After a few days, the saint was passing by when he saw the snake in an unconscious state. He understood everything though the snake did not tell him anything.
>
> The saint exclaimed, 'What a shame! You are such a fool! You don't know how to protect yourself. I asked you not to bite, but I didn't forbid you to hiss. Why didn't you scare them by hissing?'

Once the fear of snake was gone from the mind of the boys, the snake was beaten mercilessly. The only way to save his life was to create fear at least by hissing.

No Opponent Should Dare to Strike Twice

All people fear the humiliation, pain and suffering that follows defeat. Here lies the clue to creating fear in the mind of the opponent. You should enter the battlefield well-prepared, with a game plan that gives you a good chance of victory. Once you conclusively defeat your rival, you must punish him, so that he fears you and does not dare oppose you again.

The opponents must be crushed completely as Machiavelli says in *The Prince*, 'Men ought either be well treated or crushed, because they can avenge themselves of lighter injuries, of more serious ones they can't; therefore the injury that is to be done to a man ought to be of such a kind that one does not stand in fear of revenge.'

Fear must also be created in the mind of any team member who dares to oppose the leader. Otherwise, he may engage in a vicious campaign against him to garner support for himself within the team and also unite with his opponents. Leaders must identify such people before they become too big. There can be only one leader in a team. Any challenger has to be tamed lest other people also develop courage to oppose the leader. What has been done with the enemy must be done with the team member also.

Checking the opposition is only one part, a leader also needs to create loyalists within the team with whom he shares an emotional bond. Enjoying much attention and privilege, these loyalists should find no benefit in supporting the opponents. Such loyalists can ensure the safety and security of their leaders.

4

Divide and Rule for Success

Divide and rule, the politician cries; unite and lead, is watchword of the wise.
—Johann Wolfgang von Goethe

Fear for a leader is not enough. Alignments have a big role to play too. That's where the divide and rule policy comes in. Leaders have successfully employed it for long.

Divide and rule is the most ancient and well-known principle of acquiring and retaining power. Every society stands divided on several grounds. Superficially, everyone seems united—just like from an airplane, a city looks like a beautiful carpet of different shades. But when you come to the ground, you find the city divided into sectors, roads, houses, parks etc. Everywhere, people are divided. In every organisation, there are honest and dishonest; efficient and inefficient; good and evil people. The honest detest the dishonest since they make more money, enjoy greater power and perks. The dishonest also hate the honest because they fear them and see them as troublemakers. They know that there are some stupid honest people who just can't be purchased.

One honest government officer was put into a cage like an animal and left out on the city streets. Everyone stared at this 'rare animal' for it was quite difficult to find an honest person in the government in those days. A boy who passed by with his rich father saw this man being taken out in a procession.

He asked his father, 'Who is this man?'

The father replied, 'Son, he is an honest government officer. They are a very rare breed.'

'Please dad, buy one for me. I really like this guy.'

The father said in a resigned tone, 'That is the problem son. No one can buy him.'

Every society is divided on the basis of caste, religion, class, haves and have-nots. They begrudge each other, yet are forced to live in peace. If you wish to be a leader, you may have to disturb this superficial peace and make the division more clear—take a side.

When you disturb the status quo of society and force people to take a position, you should be ready to face hatred from the other group. People often try to remain neutral towards the events of the world and lead an independent life. It is possible to lead such a life, but then one should not expect any support from any side, at a time of need.

A great conflict was brewing between the birds and the beasts. When the two armies stood facing each other, the bat was not sure which one to join. The birds that passed his perch said, 'Come with us,' but he said, 'I am a beast.'

Later on, some beasts who passed underneath him, looked up and said, 'Come with us'; but he said, 'I am a bird.'

Luckily, at the last moment, peace was made, and no battle took place, so the bat came to the birds, wishing to join them in their rejoicing. But they all turned against him and he had to fly away.

He then went to the beasts, but soon had to beat a retreat, or else be torn to pieces.

'Ah,' said the bat, 'I see now. One who is neither one thing nor the other has no friends.'

Leaders cannot be neutral. They have to take a stand and take sides. Thus, they create enemies as well as friends.

Leaders Need to Take Sides Too

If you are already in a position of power, say as the head of an office, organisation or nation, you must decide your priorities by taking a side. If you side with honesty, come down heavily on dishonest people. They must be sidelined and punished so that a clear message goes out to the people. Not only must you have no sympathy for such people, but feel a sense of pride and achievement for taking on such people. You will find that all the honest people in your organisation come forward to help you. Jack Welch says, 'In such cases (integrity violations), you don't need to hesitate for a moment before firing someone, or fret about it either. Just do it, and make sure the organisation knows why, so that consequences of breaking the rules are not lost on anyone.'

You must also display the highest level of honesty and integrity to attract all honest people so that you can counter dishonest forces. But if you are yourself not honest, you will only be fighting a losing battle by choosing to side with honesty.

A policeman stops a car.

Driver: Is anything wrong, officer?

Policeman: No, we just wanted to reward you for being the hundred thousandth car driving on this new highway.

Driver: Thank god! I thought you are going to ask me for my driving license, 'cause I don't have one, you know...

Driver's wife: Don't believe anything he says. He's completely drunk!

Grandpa on the back seat: I knew we wouldn't come far with this stolen car!

Sonny from the trunk: Have we crossed the border, yet?

It is evident from the story that truth and honesty do not go hand-in-hand with illegal actions. If your deeds are not in accordance with the law, it would be foolish to try to be honest. If you seek personal gratification due to your position in the organisation, you have no option but to align yourself with the dishonest and corrupt who have similar goals and tell lies. You have to sideline the honest people and empower the dishonest.

Often leaders divide the organisation or society on the basis of caste, class, religion or race. There are always deep prejudices within every society on these lines. Consider the following:

- Poor blame the rich people for loss of property, saying that the rich have cornered all the wealth.
- The rich blame the poor for all the inefficiency, complacency and law and order issues.
- The majority blames the minority for the troubles of the nation.
- The minority blames the majority for partiality and insensitivity.

These are some of the common prejudices everywhere. A leader has to just exploit them and lead one of the groups. People are more united in fear than in love. Great leaders usually rally people behind them by uniting them against a common enemy. If there was no enemy, they invent one. Buddhist author and activist, Thich Nhat Hanh rightly warned people, 'In order to rally people, governments need enemies. They want us to be afraid, to hate, so we will rally behind them. And if they do not have a real enemy, they will invent one in order to mobilise us.'

Creating an enemy is an important strategy of leadership. When people see a great enemy whom they can't fight themselves, they desperately seek leaders who show them how to overcome this enemy.

The Positive Outcome of Dividing People

We give our best only when our survival is at stake. When everything is peaceful, we nap and enjoy life. Only when we have an adversary, we improve ourselves to meet the challenge. All the sports provide man with a platform where people can display their strengths even in times of peace. Even in colleges and schools, it is common to divide the students into different teams and make them play against each other to win trophies. Though these divisions are initially purely random, people gradually get attached to their teams and develop emotional bonding with them. In many countries, people align themselves with the league teams in football or cricket so closely that they even fight with the supporters of the opposite team, as if they were enemies fighting a war. William Shankly, a Scottish football manager once said, 'Some people believe football is a matter of life and death. I am very disappointed with that attitude. I can assure you it is much, much more important than that.'

In every democratic country, there are several political parties who fight against each other for the votes and support of people, and they too divide the society on party lines. Voters analyse the strengths and weakness of different parties and then align themselves with the party that serves their interest better.

The Arithmetic of Divide and Rule

You have to first divide people in a way that you have more people with you than any other rival. That calls for multiple divisions in the beginning. Let us say you get the support of 25 per cent of the people and 75 per cent are still against you. You have to keep the 25 per cent united behind you, and work at dividing the remaining 75 per cent. If you can again divide them to say 35 per cent and 40 per cent, then you can align with one to defeat the other, as your role becomes critical for the success of either party. Later when you get stronger, you can defeat your ally too or ask them to merge with you.

Your strength increases as you defeat your enemies one by one. When you stand unchallenged, you start consolidating and unite everyone behind you.

Thus, even though leaders start by dividing the society, ultimately they unite all. Many great nations were thus built. It was the Civil War that united the United States and made it a superpower over time. The division of Christendom into various states led to competition amongst European countries, consequently some emerged as the richest and most powerful in the world. They even fought two World Wars with each other. However, now they have come together again under the European Union.

A visionary leader does not divide the society to weaken it, but to make it stronger. He is like the surgeon who conducts a surgery not to give you pain, but actually to cure the disease and eliminate the pain. Yet, people often remember the pain of surgery more than the pain the surgery eliminates from the future.

Division itself is neither good or evil; moral or immoral; ethical or unethical. It depends on the real intention of a leader. You cannot become a powerful leader, unless you are ready to exploit the divisions within the society or organisation.

5

Why Leaders Need to Deceive

Men are so simple of mind, and so much dominated by their immediate needs, that a deceitful man will always find plenty who are ready to be deceived.

—Machiavelli

What cannot be achieved by force can often be easily gained through deception. Deception is the greatest weapon of the weak and poses the biggest danger to the powerful. It is important to learn about deception, if only to protect ourselves from those who try to deceive.

> A newly-wed couple received a number of gifts on their reception. One of the gifts was an envelope containing two tickets for a popular movie show. In the place of sender, it was written 'Guess who?'
>
> The couple attended the movie wondering who could be the sender. When they returned that night after the show, they found their house robbed. On the bare table in the dining room was a card written in the same handwriting, 'Now you know!'

Imagine that you are a new leader facing stalwarts who are well-established and have power and resources far exceeding yours. How can one person fight against an organisation, which already has thousands of followers? How can you even think of winning when the balance of power is so much against you? The only strategy is deception.

We know that the key to victory is to have accurate knowledge of the self and the enemy. Yet, if both opponents equally know each other and themselves, the benefit is neutralised. The real benefit can come only when:

- You know your enemy, but the enemy does not know you well.
- You know your enemy well, but the enemy does not know that you know him so well.
- You know your enemy well, but you ensure that your enemy knows you incorrectly.

You must be aware of what tricks your enemy might employ, but successfully conceal your own. Better still is to deceive in a way that your enemy is misled into believing what you want him to believe, and not what is true. War, in short, is a game of deception as the Chinese General Sun Tzu says,

> All warfare is based on deception. Hence, when we are able to attack, we must seem unable; when using our forces, we must appear inactive; when we are near, we must make the enemy believe we are far away; when far away, we must make him believe we are near.

In the real war, you win not merely by force, but by strategy, which includes deception. One who is too mindful of the rules of the game often loses the battle if the other party uses both power as well as deception. You can win a war without deception only when you are more powerful than your rival. Yet, power is acquired only gradually, and in the initial phase of your struggle, no leader can expect to overpower the enemy purely on the basis of strength.

The Morality of Deception

Deception is an art which needs the highest level of intelligence because it requires getting into the mind of your opponent and manipulating his thoughts. This is never a simple task. You must also ensure that you are not caught since failing in deception means very high punishment and loss of reputation. Hence, the risk is quite high when deceiving others.

> A burglar was trying to steal from a safe by opening the lock. Just then he saw a sticker on the safe proclaiming, 'The safe is open. Just move this knob.'
>
> The thief accordingly moved the knob, but it set off a loud alarm. Immediately, the police arrived and arrested the burglar. As he was being taken away, he said weeping, 'I have now lost all faith in humanity.'

The principles of morality and legality are applicable to only those who are themselves following legal and moral ways. However, to punish the deceiver and defeat him at his own game, you must use deception. As Machiavelli said, 'It is double pleasure to deceive the deceiver.' When the opponent is too strong and deceitful, you can't fight him in a straight battle.

The game of power is to avoid fighting face-to-face. When you expose your methods and strategies to your opponents, you are already weakened by half and the enemy becomes doubly stronger. Your success comes easily when you see the enemy very clearly but the enemy can't see you as you have hidden yourself.

Like diamond cuts diamond, a deceiver is better placed to recognise and defeat another. If your profession is about checking crime, you seek the support of criminals who have an axe to grind against other law breakers. Acting as informers, these criminals can help the police track criminals. Any civil society will find it tough to survive unless it can pay back evil in the same coin. Deceivers can be exposed only through deception.

While the advocates of morality, legality and ethics spend much time delving into the immorality of actions, a leader tries to defeat his opponents in the easiest possible way. His logic is: Even if the enemy can be conquered, why fight him when you can simply intimidate him, or win by deception? That saves so much of time, energy and lives. Such actions are bound to be criticised by intellectuals who concern themselves more with the means than the end. Leaders, however, need to produce results and fulfil their promises.

If you use deception for self-interest, it may be evil. But if it is done for a greater purpose and in the best interest of humanity, it is a big sacrifice one makes, for it is not easy to bear the brunt of criticism that comes in its wake.

Learning to Deceive

Deception is all about appearing what you are not. If you are an enemy, you must seem like a friend. If you are a friend, act like the enemy. When you are weak, project your strength so that the enemy hesitates to fight you and you get sufficient time to make yourself stronger. On the contrary, if you are strong, appear weak, so that your enemy becomes an aggressor and expects a quick victory and you then turn the tables. One of the greatest deceptions is to look foolish when you are intelligent, and look simple when you are cunning. Read the story of this boy:

> A boy used to stand in the street on market-days and let people point out that he was as an idiot. No matter how often people offered him a large and a small coin, he always chose the smaller one.

One day a kind man said to him, 'Dear son, you should take the bigger coin. Then you will have more money and people will no longer be able to make a laughing stock out of you.'

'That may be true,' said the boy. 'But if I always take the larger coin, people will stop offering me money to prove that I am more idiotic than they are. Then I would have no money at all.'

Mahatma Gandhi lived like a poor man, wearing only a loincloth. So much so, that when he visited England in 1930, Winston Churchill refused to meet him calling him 'a half-naked fakir'. Yet, it was quite an expensive affair to create the aura of poverty around him, which became his trademark. Sarojini Naidu, one of the key leaders of Congress had aptly remarked once how much it cost to keep Mahatma Gandhi in poverty. No wonder the poor, powerless and illiterate considered him their leader and one of them, while actually he was one of the most educated, powerful and resourceful persons of his time.

You may call him a deceiver but most people call him a great leader.

6

Cover Your Evil

People who claim that they're evil are usually no worse than the rest of us.... It's people who claim that they're good or any way better than the rest of us that you have to be wary of.

—Gregory Maguire

Hiding what you are is but an act of deception too. As it is important for a leader to keep up appearances, he must reveal only the good and hide that which may not be considered so.

The truth is often bitter and concealed from people. Author and humourist, Mark Twain wisely said, 'Clothes make the man. Naked people have little or no influence on society.' Your reputation is like your brand new clothes which are shining when used for the first time. However, they tend to get dirty with your sweat, dust in the atmosphere and the things which you come in contact while doing your job. You have to launder them regularly to keep them shining. If the shirt gets a blot due to contact with some dirty object, oil or chemical which can't be removed, it is better to discard the soiled shirt and wear a new one to maintain the smart image.

No leader can be effective if his people know him as well as they know their close friends and family. The mystery of leadership is created only by covering all the evils in a leader and highlighting only his strengths.

Only Half the Story is Told

With partial revelation of truth, everything can be made beautiful and glamorous. Even killing of human beings, which is so painful and inhuman can be depicted as an admirable act, when the bitterness of reality is left out. But how many actually have the heart to see thousands butchered in war? Can they see innocent men, women and children killed alongside soldiers? The complete story is different from half-truths.

Reality is bitter and needs to be concealed from the public because most people are not mature or courageous enough to face it. One of the major reasons why America lost the war with Vietnam was the exposure of the horrors of war to the common man.

> The Vietnam War was a television war. The number of television channels and broadcasts during the Vietnam War worldwide was so much more than in the whole of World War II. Everybody was notified, told and sometimes, manipulated which caused the Peace Protest in America and supporting countries, such as UK and Australia. The world had their eyes on the war; they saw the pictures, clips and voice recordings of how the war was conducted, and how cruelly the Vietnamese locals were killed.

Though many movies across the world glorify war and advocate it as a solution, only one who has seen war knows the reality. Dwight D Eisenhower, the thirty-fourth president of the United States, who was a five-star general in the US army during WWII said, 'I hate war as only a soldier who has lived it can, only as one who has seen its brutality, its futility, its stupidity.'

Good leaders must learn to conceal the brutalities, manipulations and dirty tricks from public glare. Just like you cannot admire a soldier if you see him killing brutally in the war-field, people may not love or respect their leader if they learn his complete truth.

Leaders conceal unsavoury bits to project the nice picture people want to see. But they have to be extremely smart to conceal the truth under the cover of a beautiful lie, because when their lie is exposed, they lose all credibility.

Franklin Delano Roosevelt, popularly known as FDR, was one of the most popular presidents of United States. He led United States in the time of WWII and is credited for taking United States out of the great worldwide economic depression. He maintained the reputation of honesty and fairness in the eyes of the American people who elected him four times as he served as president from March 1933 to his death in April 1945. Yet, he was not as clean as people believed, only smart enough to use his secretary Louis Howe to cover his mistakes. Alfred B Rollins (Jr) writes in his book *Roosevelt and Howe*:

> After 1912, it was impossible to think of either Roosevelt or Howe without the other. They operated as part of one political personality. They complemented each other in strengths and weaknesses. With smiles and warmth for both of them, genial Roosevelt specialised in the high level generalisation, in persuasive speeches and personal charm in public contacts, and in broad questions of public policy. Sardonic, cynical, shrewd and chronically suspicious and worried, Louis Howe concentrated on secret manoeuvre, the manipulation of the press, the organisation of personal loyalties and patronage hunger. ...And he proved to be a convenient scapegoat for their mutual error. Howe could arrange, Roosevelt confirm. Roosevelt could absorb the credit and Howe the blame. But between themselves, they understood that they rose and fall together.

The Art of Scapegoating

A leader is as ordinary a person as any one of us. He errs as any of us does. He has weaknesses as all of us. Yet, he seems great because his weaknesses and failings are concealed or shifted onto someone else like Louis Howe. These people are called scapegoats.

Scapegoat is a person or group that is made to bear blame for others. According to the Old Testament, on the Day of Atonement, a priest would confess all the sins of Israelites over the head of a goat and then drive it into the wilderness, symbolically bearing their sins away. This was a convenient and painless method to free the entire population of all sins.

As already discussed in earlier chapters, good and evil are so intimately interconnected with each other that you can't have one without the other. Hence, when a leader tries to do any good work, he can't escape evil which follows the good. If good and evil are weighed together, they may balance out each other. However, like man focuses on pain more than pleasure, people focus more on the evil consequences of action rather than focusing on the good that the action brought them. The only way to perform your work efficiently without soiling your image with the evil is to find a convenient scapegoat who can take all your sins away while you remain virtuous all the time.

A leader has to deal with all types of people, some of them are so extremely evil that they need to be crushed rather than attempted to be reformed. Just like only diamond can cut diamond, only evil can overcome evil. Hence, leaders need even more extreme evil to crush the evil which may spoil the clean reputation of leaders. Consider the following example taken from *The Prince*:

> Cesare Borgia managed to take control of Romagna, in northern Italy in the year 1500. The region was ruled by petty tyrants, who had devoted themselves to plundering their subjects rather

than governing them. There was total lawlessness and the whole area was ruled by robbers and feuding families.

Cesare appointed a lieutenant general—Remirro de Orco, who was a cruel, no-nonsense man, and gave him complete control of the region. Orco pacified and united the area using brutal force and soon got rid of all the lawless elements. However, soon people started hating him for using brute force against them. At this point, the cesare decided that such draconian powers were no longer necessary and might cause resentment. ...He decided to show that if the regime had been cruel, that was due to the brutal nature of Remirro, not to him. So as soon as he found a pretext, he had de Orco beheaded and his corpse put on display one morning in the piazza in Cesena with a wooden block and a bloody knife beside. The ferocity of the spectacle left people both gratified and shocked.

Every clever leader must keep ready scapegoats to shift their errors and blunders onto. They should never be seen as imperfect due to any visible defects in them. Baltasar Gracian, a Spanish Jesuit, baroque prose writer and philosopher wisely said, 'Folly consists not in committing folly, but in being incapable of concealing it. All men make mistakes, but the wise conceal the blunders that have been made, while fools make them public. Reputation depends more on what is hidden than on what is seen. If you can't be good, be careful.'

We see leaders using scapegoats all the time. The government in power almost invariably blames opposition, crony capitalism, judiciary, press and bureaucracy for all the problems. Whenever they are found on the wrong foot or engaged in corruption, they conveniently make some junior minister the scapegoat and remove him from power while secretly supporting him for keeping quiet. Once the matter is forgotten, the same minister comes back to power.

The business leaders whose organisations are losing market often blame their competitors for following illegal and unethical means to succeed and government policies for their failures. They often sack some employee as a scapegoat, blaming him for all the problems.

If a leader can't shift the blame convincingly and fails to maintain the image of impeccable integrity and efficiency, that is the beginning of the end of his leadership.

PART IV

THE FACADE OF A LEADER

1

A Pleasant Personality

I knew that I had come face to face with someone whose mere personality was so fascinating that, if I allowed it to do so, it would absorb my whole nature, my whole soul, my very art itself.

—Oscar Wilde

Leaders have never been the epitome of virtues as they have many negative qualities in them like excessive desire, unbridled ambition, hunger for power, ruthlessness and deception. These are present in all of us too, but perhaps they are in excess in leaders, as from these evils, leaders develop their great virtues. However, not many understand the intimate connection between good and evil. Hence, leaders have to create a facade to cover the evil.

Leaders must appear not what they are, but what people wish to see in an ideal leader.

In order to attract others, a leader must have an attractive personality. It is not without reason that heroes and heroines in books and movies have attractive and pleasant personalities. It is not that ordinary-looking people lack courage, intelligence or that they don't love—but no producer would like to cast an unattractive man or woman as a hero or heroine in his film. The audience is unlikely to spend their money and time to see people who are unattractive or ordinary looking. They need idols they can admire. Mae West, an American actress, singer, playwright and screenwriter said, 'Personality is the glitter that sends your little gleam across the footlights and the orchestra pit into that big black space where the audience is.'

Leaders have to sell themselves to their followers and good packaging is an absolute must to attract the attention of the customers. The polishing, finishing and the colours of any item like car, refrigerator and mobile phone actually play no role in enhancing the performance of the item, yet they are extremely important in selling the product. Leaders too must develop a great exterior to be liked by the people. LeRoy Neiman, an American artist known for his brilliantly coloured, expressionist paintings and screen prints of athletes, musicians and sporting events said, 'When I paint, I seriously consider the public presence of a person—the surface facade. I am less concerned with how people look when they wake up or how they act at home. A person's public presence reflects his own efforts at image development.'

Who knew this better than Steve Jobs, the founder and the CEO of Apple Inc.? He believed that computers should not merely be useful, but also beautiful and even the packaging must be attractive. Jonathan Ive, the senior vice president of design at Apple Inc, who designed many of Apple's products, including the MacBook Pro, iMac, MacBook Air, iPod, iPod Touch, iPhone, iPad, iPad Mini and iOS 7 said, 'Steve and I spend a lot of time on the packaging. I love the process of unpacking something. You design a ritual of unpacking to make the product feel special. Packaging can be theatre, it can create a story.'

In fact, among the patents that Jobs and Ive shared, there were several designs of iPod and iPhone boxes. Altogether, Job's name would appear on three hundred and thirteen Apple patents covering clasps, designs, power cords and that graceful glass staircase. The boxes are so elegant that some fans can't part with them, storing them in wardrobes or displaying them on shelves.

It is a fact that most people judge a book by its cover and the title. While the inner content of the book is important, it is also equally important to have an attractive cover page to attract the readers. An attractive cover ensures that the customers at least open and see what is inside. It is wisely said, 'Personality has the power to open many doors, but character must keep them open.'

Hence, a leader must develop a pleasing personality to create the magnetism and the charisma that pulls others towards him or her.

1. Maintain Physical Fitness

A leader should maintain good health and fitness. The body, mind and soul are integral parts of the human personality and complement each other. No one wants to see a sick or unfit person at the helm of affairs.

2. Choose Your Attire Carefully

How you dress determines your personality. We may not realise, but we are constantly judged by how we dress and look. Informal dressing reveals the casual attitude of a leader while formal dressing projects a savvy and professional image. When Gandhi joined the Indian freedom struggle, he changed his attire in line with his new calling. Discarding the formal jacket of an attorney, he dressed then in just a loincloth with no upper garment. His simplicity struck an immediate chord with the poor and illiterate in India, who could identify with their leader. Even though he was highly educated and commanded the Congress party which had no dearth of wealth, Gandhi's simplistic dressing made all the difference in making him the leader of the masses. The requirement of the job thus dictates the dress sense of a leader.

Major CA Mach instructed the graduating student-officers of the Second Training Camp at Fort Sheridan in 1917, as following:

> It is exceedingly difficult for an officer to be dignified while wearing a dirty, spotted uniform and a three days' stubble of whiskers on his face. Such a man lacks self-respect, and self-respect is an essential of dignity.
>
> There may be occasions when your work entails dirty clothes and an unshaved face. Your men all look that way. At such times there is ample reason for your appearance. In fact, it would be a mistake to look too clean—they would think that you were not doing your share. But as soon as this unusual occasion has passed, set an example for personal neatness.

Our dressing helps us convey our message in the most subtle way, concealing and exposing as we desire. You must dress appropriately to convey the right message to your people.

3. A Positive Body Language Pays

The posture and body language of a person can reveal the mind of the person. A confident person usually stands erect and moves straight, while a wavering person is restless. A depressed, disappointed and pessimistic person tends to look down while walking, but an optimist looks up and meets the eye when he walks.

The renowned martial arts expert, Morihei Ueshiba said, 'A good stance and posture reflect a proper state of mind.' Leaders win the game not merely by fighting, but mostly by posturing. When you change your posture, you also change your state of mind as the two are intimately connected. In the words of Dale Carnegie, the author of the international bestseller *How to Win Friends and Influence People*, 'The expression one wears on one's face is far more important than the clothes one wears on one's back.'

Is not a beautiful smile the best way to project a pleasant personality?

You can win the heart of even your greatest opponent sometimes with just a smile that comes from your heart. Dale Carnegie adds, 'An insincere grin? No. That doesn't fool anybody. We know it is mechanical and we resent it. I am talking about a real smile, a heart-warming smile, a smile that comes from within, the kind of smile that will bring a good price in the marketplace.'

4. Get Interested in Others

Instead of waiting for people to walk up to them, leaders approach people to know them better so that they can help them achieve their aspirations. Carnegie said, 'You can make more friends in two months by becoming interested in other people than you can in two years by trying to get other people interested in you.'

Leaders are not pleasant because they are handsome or good-looking, but because they please people who come in contact with them. As James Allen, the British philosopher pointed out, 'Men do not attract that which they want, but that which they are.' You tend to attract pleasant company when you are amiable. If you act unpleasantly, you attract likewise. The company of such unpleasant people may eventually destroy your leadership. You are avoided by people not only because of who you are, but also because of the company you keep.

We cannot please and attract people merely with a warm handshake, pleasant words and false smiles. There must be genuine liking and compassion. If you have negative feelings for others, your negative vibes are bound to reach them and repel. The only way to become attractive is to be positive towards those whom you wish to attract.

The secret of liking others is not very complex. We know that when we like a person, we tend to see only the positives and not the negatives. If you dislike most people in the world, it is because you have trained yourself to see only the negative in people. Change the way you look at people to create the feeling of love in you. As African American poet Maya Angelou said, 'If you train your mind to search for the positive things about other people, you will be surprised at how many good things you can observe in them and comment upon.'

Once you train your mind to see the positive, you will not only start liking so many people, but also build a personality that is liked by many people.

5. Cultivate the Art of Careful Communication

Leaders are invariably great at communicating their message across. Some like Churchill and Hitler were known for their oratory, which gave them tremendous power to motivate their people. Yet, other leaders like Gandhi communicated more through their actions than their words.

In order to communicate well, leaders must develop synergy in their thoughts, words and actions. As thoughts keep changing, one must know how to control the mind and in turn, words. It's best to avoid saying something which would expose your ignorance. Former US President Abraham Lincoln famously said, 'Better to remain silent and be thought a fool than to speak out and remove all doubt.' As a matter of fact, if you speak less, you are likely to be considered wiser. Learn to weigh every word before you speak, as your words and actions are closely watched by many people. And it is dangerous for leaders to go back on what they have said or promised.

6. Self-Respect

How attractive a leader is, is often gauged by the respect he commands from his followers. Yet, before we expect others to respect us, we must learn to respect our own self. Dr Joyce Brothers, an American psychologist, television personality and columnist said, 'An individual's self-concept is the core of his personality. It affects every aspect of human behaviour: The ability to learn, the capacity to grow and change. A strong, positive self-image is the best possible preparation for success in life.'

It is not easy to create a great self-image because we are aware of our evil self. We can fool others by showing only our good side, but it is impossible to fool our own self. Hence, in order to develop a good self-image, we must actually strive to be good by increasing our good deeds and reducing evil thoughts and deeds.

The Hindu scripture *Yajurveda* states that attractiveness and magnetism of man's personality is the result of his inner radiance. Good deeds fill our inner self with radiance and glory that make us special and worthy of the genuine respect in the minds of others.

When leaders develop pleasant personalities, people like being around them as it makes them feel more positive. Their pessimism evaporates as they develop hope and start seeing the world in a new light, which is good and full of glory.

7. Sense of Humour

A good sense of humour makes a leader appear affable and charming. A leader who can make you smile is always acceptable. Humour comes more readily to positive people. A leader full of grudges may find it difficult to laugh with his people. Many great leaders like Mahatma Gandhi, Winston Churchill, Abraham Lincoln and Ronald Reagan are remembered even today for their sense of humour. Ronald Reagan used humour effectively to complain without being bitter. At the fundraising rally for William Lucas in Detroit, Michigan on 24 September 1986, Reagan was at his wittiest best:

> There was a kid standing outside a Democratic fundraising dinner. And as those in attendance filed out, he started hawking them and he told us, he had puppies.
>
> He held them up and gave the pitch, 'Democrat puppies for sale. Anybody want a Democrat puppy?'
>
> Two weeks later, the Republicans happened to hold a fundraiser at the same restaurant. And there was the same kid with the

same batch of puppies. Only this time, his pitch was changed, 'Republican puppies for sale. Anyone want to buy a Republican puppy?'

A reporter noticed that the same kid had been at the other meeting too, so he said, 'Wait a minute, kid. How come this same bunch of puppies were Democratic puppies two weeks ago, and now they're Republicans?'

The kid did not falter even for a minute, and said, 'Now their eyes have opened.'

A good sense of humour makes a leader quite attractive and pleasant as we all wish to be in the company of people who can make us forget our problems, at least for some time.

2

Be an Actor

Acting deals with very delicate emotions. It is not putting up a mask. Each time an actor acts he does not hide; he exposes himself.

—Rodney Dangerfield

Leaders should not only 'act' and be seen as 'acting', but they must also be great 'actors'. They have to not only 'perform' as in work, but actually put up a 'performance' to convince people. Leaders are so closely watched, their every action is so closely observed that it is essential for them to put up an act so that people continue to believe in them. When people believe their leaders, they also follow all their actions.

When we watch a movie that has a great script and acting, we often become a part of that experience, crying at emotional scenes and getting charged up in action sequences. When our hero is beaten by the villain, we curse the villain who may actually be a good man in real life. Despite knowing that it is all fiction and people are just acting, we mirror its emotions, responding as if it were real.

If a movie act can influence people in such a way, what could not be done if you act well in your real life? And that too when people do not know that you are acting. This is exactly why a great leader is one who can put up a great act. Leaders entertain, inform and convince people through their dialogues, action and drama. Some people consider oration as the most important quality in a leader, but Churchill, who was one of the greatest orators, did not think so.

> Winston Churchill was once asked, 'Doesn't it thrill you, Mr Churchill, to know that every time you make a speech, the hall is packed to overflowing?'
>
> 'It's quite flattering,' Winston replied, 'but whenever I feel this way, I always remember that if instead of making a political speech, I was being hanged, the crowd would be twice as big.'

Churchill was wise as he knew that people like different genres of movies like comedy, action and even, tragedy. Going by that, leaders have to be not just actors, but versatile actors. For most people, leaders are favourite subjects of discussion, whom we love to praise, idolise, curse and ridicule. But for our leaders, the world would be quite a colourless and dull place.

Actors perform on-screen; leaders are expected to perform in reality. That's because of the image they carry. This image is what bonds them with their people. Most of this image is carefully cultivated. And people get swayed by all the rhetoric, not realising that it's all a part of image-building. They then expect a leader to perform wonders like the heroes do on-screen.

On 4 June 1940, during WWII, Churchill rejuvenated the British people with one of the finest speeches given in the House of Commons.

> Even though large tracts of Europe and many old and famous states have fallen or may fall into the grip of the Gestapo and all the odious apparatus of Nazi rule, we shall not flag or fail.

We shall go on to the end. We shall fight in France, we shall fight on the seas and oceans, we shall fight with growing confidence and growing strength in the air, we shall defend our island, whatever the cost may be. We shall fight on the beaches, we shall fight on the landing grounds, we shall fight in the fields and in the streets, we shall fight in the hills; we shall never surrender.

What a speech! The island nation was charged by his speech. The next year, American journalist HR Knickerbocker wrote that the words of the speech deserve to be memorised by us all, observing that, 'With Churchill's picture, these words are placarded in homes and offices throughout the British Empire.'

This speech of Churchill's can easily put to shame the greatest dialogue writers of movies. Such was the influence of the speech that every British was charged up with emotion and enthusiasm to fight and ultimately defeat the Axis forces of WWII.

Emotional Intelligence

Author and leadership expert, Dale Carnegie advised many decades ago, 'When dealing with people, let us remember we are not dealing with creatures of logic. We are dealing with creatures of emotion, creatures bristling with prejudices and motivated by pride and vanity.' The role of emotional intelligence in leadership is now well-recognised. However, unlike knowledge, emotions cannot be learned except by personal experience.

We do not understand pain unless we ourselves suffer it. And as we try to avoid all forms of pain in our life, we remain ignorant of many such emotions. Similarly, there are many pleasures that come with achievements alone. For example, to feel like a prime minister, you have to become a prime minister. Though everyone wishes to know these emotions of pleasure, only a few actually achieve the positions that accord them with these emotions. Like an actor, a leader develops emotional intelligence.

For an actor, display of emotion is just part of the job. Irrespective of whether a hero has acted as a dying man or a king or a joker or a heartbroken lover, his family members may not know since when he comes home, he does not suffer from any of those emotions. As soon as the shot is over, the actor changes his emotion of a weeping lover to a cheerful man that he is. He lives through the emotions only till the camera lights are on. After the act is over, he is back to his natural self. Yet, when he acts, he puts his heart and soul into the acting.

Most actors, due to their act of passing through different emotions can become emotionally intelligent or even emotionally fragile. The former can become great leaders while the latter lead a miserable life. Emotional intelligence can thus transform actors into leaders, and leaders into great leaders.

The On-screen and Off-screen Fiction

Through his words and deeds, a leader triggers the imagination of his people. He sells them dreams for a better future, more fruitful life and a safer world.

There is tremendous similarity between leaders and actors. They promise to do all the hard work for fulfilling your dreams. This may be illogical but that is what they sell, and that is what you and I wish to believe. In reality, they may be realising their own dreams. An entrepreneur tells his customers that he is working to meet their demand—their dreams of acquiring better products and services at lowest price, while in reality, he is trying to realise his own dream of making it big.

Unless you are a great actor, it is difficult to carry on the job of being a leader for long. A leader's role is in fact tougher than that of an actor. It is not as important for an actor to be what he is perceived to be by the public, as long as his acting is good.

The Pain of a Leader

A leader sells hope to those who have none just as a businessman sells his goods to one who needs it. A leader thus appeals more to those who are poor, weak, helpless and suffering; those who have little hope of making it on their own. They are often not doers or hard workers, but constantly complain and expect others to solve their problems and work for them. The bane of a leader thus is that the segment that rallies behind him the most can also pull him down the most.

Most people need the government or someone else to take the blame for all their failures. This provides them psychological satisfaction that they are right. This is what former US President Ronald Reagan once said:

> I remember a story back from my Jim Rhodes days, my governor days in California. I was on the way to the office one morning, had the car radio on. And there was a disc jockey playing songs and so forth, and suddenly, I heard him saying—now, we were having some problems at the time—I heard him saying something that endeared him to me.
>
> He said, 'Every man should take unto himself a wife, because sooner or later, something is bound to happen that you can't blame on the governor.'

If you are really a hard worker, you can get over your problems sooner or later with your sincerity and commitment. However, instead of solving their issues, people who choose to blame everyone else, seldom overcome their problems. A leader who empathises with them in the true sense is bound to suffer like them.

Therefore, a wise leader 'acts' before such supporters and does not actually take up the burden of their problems. He knows that if he tells these people the truth and asks them to work harder, be positive and look within, they would instantly discard him as a leader.

Unless you are a great actor, you cannot empathise with them and get their support.

A hero's romantic antics look very good on screen, but such dancing and singing in public places is impractical and laughable, and never happens in real life. Also, a real life police officer does not kill criminals at the drop of a hat or torture them at will in police custody like the heroic officer does in movies. All this is blatantly illegal, for which he can be dismissed from service and even be tried for murder.

A great leader knows that people are more often than not selfish and naive. However, instead of choosing to make them wiser by imparting true knowledge, he acts as per their fantasy and provides hope. He knows that these hopes may not be realised and so has a ready explanation prepared beforehand.

> Once Churchill was asked by a journalist, 'Please tell us what qualities an aspiring politician should have?'
>
> 'Well,' replied Churchill, 'First of all, he must have the knack to foretell what will take place tomorrow, next week, next month and year.'
>
> Then after a pause he added, 'Besides, he should have the ability to explain why these haven't happened.'

Entertain like Actors

Author and motivational speaker, Tony Robbins remarks, 'We aren't in an information age; we are in an entertainment age.' Entertainment is extremely important in modern life. Entertainment means something that amuses, pleases or diverts our attention for some time. Arts in all forms like movies and fiction serve this purpose. Billions of books on fiction are sold every year around the world, far more than the books on self-help, philosophy, spirituality, religion and every other topic that tries to explain the truth. So a leader must learn to entertain. People are not entertained only when we say nice things or speak the truth.

Often, they enjoy painting someone a villain, for this not just makes them look like heroes, but also gives them a punching bag towards whom they direct all their ire. A successful leader frequently has to fulfil such untrue and unrealistic wishes of the people.

If you observe, you will find that a movie has all types of villains like politicians, rich men and even policemen. But a common man is always shown to be right, notwithstanding the fact that they too may be committing crimes, and that they themselves elect the leaders whom they love to hate. Customers and voters are always right and a true leader must never say anything negative about them.

A leader must learn to not only get into the skin of the character but also into the hearts of his people to know what they want. Instead of dwelling on weaknesses, he should highlight their strengths to develop confidence and affection, and then gradually try to work on their weaknesses. He needs to play upon their imagination and satisfy their dreams. Not only must he try to change people through his performance, but also change his act according to the requirements of the people.

A leader through his acting gradually develops true emotions as our actions and feelings are interconnected. Just like our emotions drive our actions, our actions create corresponding emotions. Good leaders, thus, gradually develop genuine sympathy for their people and work to improve their lives with sincerity and dedication.

3

The Propaganda War

Through clever and constant application of propaganda, people can be made to see paradise as hell, and also the other way round, to consider the most wretched sort of life as paradise.

—*Adolf Hitler*

'No matter how big the lie,' said former US President John F Kennedy, 'Repeat it often enough and the masses will regard it as the truth.' We have seen that a leader needs to act, sometimes deceive, sometimes conceal and present a façade too. To sell all this and more, he also wages the propaganda war. Propaganda has been universally recognised as a powerful tool for success in politics and leadership. It works like advertisement does for business. Propaganda not only makes one more popular, but can also demolish the reputation of others. No leader can afford to ignore the power of propaganda.

A reputed expert in public relations, Edward L Bernays writes in his book *Propaganda*,

> It is asked whether, in fact, the leader makes propaganda, or

whether propaganda makes the leader. There is a widespread impression that a good press agent can puff up a nobody into a great man.

The answer is the same as that made to the old query as to whether the newspaper makes public opinion or whether public opinion makes the newspaper. There has to be fertile ground for the leader and the idea to fall on. But the leader also has to have some vital seed to sow. To use another figure, a mutual need has to exist before either can become positively effective. Propaganda is of no use to the politician unless he has something to say which the public, consciously or unconsciously, wants to hear.'

And the public wants to hear a lot about the people who are powerful and wealthy. They are interested not only in their success, but also in their failures. Since there are few successes and more failures, negative propaganda often works better than the positive one.

There are several forms of propaganda. Some are overt while others are covert. Leaders use both to achieve their desired objective.

1. Using Rumour as a Weapon

Rumours are one of the best weapons of propaganda. You need not spend any money for spreading a rumour nor do you have to prove the truth. People are always interested in rumours, particularly the dark side of others and especially when it concerns a reputed person. When rumours are spread, everyone adds spice to them and when a rumour runs for long, it seems real.

> One day Mullah Nasruddin and his friends decided to play a joke on the people in a village. So Nasruddin drew a crowd, and lied to them about a gold mine in a certain place.
>
> When everybody ran to get their hands on the gold, Nasruddin started running with them.

> When asked by his friends why he was following them, he said, 'So many people believed it, that I think it might be true!'

Usually people verify a rumour by cross-checking it, but if the rumour is widespread, and everyone knows it, cross verification becomes impossible.

Repeated ill rumours kill reputation, like termites which eat into the grandest buildings and tallest trees, for they make people suspicious of their leader. Most people reason that there must have been some truth in the rumour to have set it going.

Once a rumour acquires momentum, everyone believes it till it is proven otherwise. Spreading a negative rumour may be one of the best ways to beat the enemy. Once it spreads, the enemy is in double jeopardy: If they defend themselves, people are disinclined to believe them; if they keep quiet, people take the rumour to be true.

It's like answering the question, 'Do you still beat your wife?'

You can't say 'yes' or 'no'.

2. Negative Campaigning Too Pays at Times

Life is often a zero sum game. When the market share of your competitors goes down, your share automatically goes up. So if you spoil the image of your opponent, your image becomes much cleaner. A leader may then question: Why should he waste so much energy in improving his own performance when the same job can be accomplished by easier means? Take this example:

> Two politicians were discussing their strategies.
>
> The Democrat said, 'Whenever I take a cab, I give the cabbie a large tip and say, "Vote for Democrats".'
>
> The Republican said, 'Whenever I take a cab, I don't give any tip to the driver and say, "Vote for Democrats".'

So one can, at times, use negative campaigning to defeat their rivals without spending a penny.

In any society, though many wish to reach the top, few are successful in achieving their dream. The general propensity of the people then is to blame someone else for their failures. A clever leader exploits this human weakness to hold his opponent accountable for all the failures of his people. This type of campaign may be false, yet people believe it readily as they want to believe it. Tremendous hatred for the opponent can be fanned in the minds of the people by a prolonged vicious campaign.

3. Advertisements Can Project a Positive Image

Advertisements help influence public opinion positively. The effect of advertisements is slow but sure. When you publicise your strengths repeatedly, gradually people believe them. The best advertisements are however those which are disguised as news. President Ronald Reagan gave this message thus:

> You know, some people think there's a storm brewing between me and the news industry. That simply isn't true. My feelings about the media haven't changed a bit. No. No. No, I have always been and always will be in complete agreement with Thomas Jefferson on this subject. He said, 'If it were left to me to decide whether we should have a government without newspapers or newspapers without a government, I should not hesitate a moment to prefer the latter.' Of course, he also said, 'Perhaps the editor might divide his paper into four chapters, heading the first "truth"; second "probabilities"; third "possibilities"; fourth "lies".'

4. Use the Vehicle of Propaganda

Douglas MacArthur said, 'One can't wage war under present conditions without the support of public opinion, which is tremendously moulded by the press and other forms of propaganda.' One may hate media when they are reporting against you, but you can't live without them.

When used effectively, propaganda can demolish the enemy without firing a single shot. If the opponents are weakened and demoralised before the actual battle starts, they become an easy prey to attack.

4

Leadership Branding

Unless you have absolute clarity of what your brand stands for, everything else is irrelevant.

—*Mark Baynes*

'What's in a name?' said William Shakespeare, 'that which we call a rose by any other name would smell as sweet.' He was right as he was referring to a flower created by nature, whose name has been assigned by man. However, in case of individuals, leaders and organisation, names matter a lot. The name of a person represents the complete philosophy of the person. Mahatma Gandhi, Gautama Buddha, Adolf Hitler, Abraham Lincoln, Bill Gates or Barack Obama are not simply names. Each name is a brand—representing a style of leadership.

We realise the importance of brands when buying a product; reputed brands command high prices compared to unknown or less popular ones. In a world of consumerism, when the same type of good is produced by thousands of manufacturers and similar services are provided by millions of service providers, the importance of brand can't be overemphasised.

Forbes has calculated the value for the top brands in this world, which puts Apple at the top, with a brand value of $104.3 billion, followed by Microsoft–$56.7 billion, Coca-Cola–$54.9 billion, IBM–$50.7 billion, and Google–$47.3 billion.

Branding, which is an important means to create a successful corporation, can also be used for creating successful leaders.

The Brand of a Leader

In the world where everyone is trying to be a leader, people can't follow everyone. When we think so much before buying even soap or toothpaste, we naturally think many times more before we follow another person. Being a follower means surrendering our free will to another person, which is as difficult as giving full power of attorney of all your assets to a person. Unless you trust your leader, you can't follow him.

Let us understand what a brand really is. It is a connection that a product company or service provider seeks to create with the buyer, who builds loyalty based on his emotional perception of the same.

The brand of a leader is not really rational, but emotional. When you develop emotional bonding with someone, you stop weighing the positive and negative traits of the person because that person becomes so unique to you that you are unwilling to settle for any substitute. Such is the power of emotion that you may never try another brand of the product, and hence, never know if anything outshines your favourite brand.

How many of us even think of changing our religion even if another religion is proven to be better than ours?

Hence, unless something really goes absolutely wrong with the brand you trust and love, you are unlikely to discard it.

A leader too can create a brand, which may get him many loyal followers.

Steps for Creating a Brand

1. BE A GREAT FOLLOWER

We all wish to lead and not follow anyone. That is the reason why there are hardly any books on followership while there are innumerable books on leadership. Whenever someone tries to lead us, we get quite suspicious about that person because we don't wish to be used for somebody else's success. While all leaders claim that they wish to lead us for our benefit, we find it difficult to trust them as our experience teaches us that leaders usually use their followers for their own selfish purposes.

Trust cannot be built in a short time as most of us have suffered many betrayals. It may take years to trust someone deeply. When a leader tries to lead, he is a new person for us. Why should we believe him? Recall that the relationship between a follower and a leader is an emotional one which arises from feelings that come from our deepest consciousness, over which we have little control.

It is, however, easier to connect with other followers for they are like our brothers and sisters, searching for a common goal.

A leader too can strive to relate to us thus. If a leader begins to follow some divine principle or a popular hero who is also deeply trusted by the people, we are unlikely to have any difficulty trusting him as he too is seeking the same goal. Hence, a leader successfully attracts many followers, when he adopts some higher principle, which is in the heart of many people. Once a communion between a leader and follower is established, trust sets in.

2. SIMPLE MISSION STATEMENT WORKS BEST

> There was a king who loved his people very much. He had many wise nobles as consul. One day he called all his wise nobles and asked them to pen down all their wisdom for the future generation.

The wise nobles worked for a year and put forth all their knowledge in twelve volumes of a book. When the king saw their collective work, he said, 'It is too big. Make it smaller.'

The wise nobles worked for another year and condensed their wisdom to just one volume and presented it to the king. The king again said, 'It is too big. Make it smaller.'

So they worked for yet another year, and finally reduced the entire wisdom to one single page and presented it to the king. The king complimented them for their work, but said again, 'Make it even smaller.'

Finally, the nobles reduced the entire wisdom to just one phrase and the king was extremely happy. He said, 'That is what people can understand.'

The phrase read—'There is no free lunch!'

It is extremely difficult for a common person to understand the complex philosophy and thoughts of a leader. The wider the appeal a leader craves, the more he must simplify his message. Who can forget Barack Obama's election slogan, 'Yes. We Can.'

Even companies simplify their vision and mission to just a line. The punchline, 'Think Different' reminds us of Apple Macintosh for their emphasis on innovation and uniqueness. The entire concept of *Upanishads* can be simplified in just one line: *Aham Brahmasmi*—I am like God, and the entire theme of Bhagawad Gita can be summarised in just two words: *Nishkama Karma*—Selfless Action.

When our focus is wide, our intensity is low. When we talk about too many things, people get confused and our energy gets dissipated in many directions. Leaders, therefore, keep one great concept at the centre and build every other concept around it. Thus, their supporters can identify their leader simply and accurately, by that one single concept.

3. BRAND BUILDING FOR LEADERS

Once leaders identify the single purpose which can describe them, they make all efforts to build that brand. Gandhi stood for truth and non-violence, and gave his life for it. He was respected for it and was also condemned for it, but he never left his principles. Hitler, who stood for racism, convinced the German people that they belonged to the most superior race in the world. Using this slogan, he emerged as their most powerful leader who made Germany the most powerful nation during WWII. Lincoln stood for black-emancipation and FD Roosevelt for development. Recently, Narendra Modi became the prime minister of India, on the single plank of 'development for all'.

Every leader must choose the followers they wish to represent and lead in business or politics. Abraham Lincoln once said, 'You can please some of the people some of the time; all of the people some of the time; some of the people all of the time, but you can never please all of the people all of the time.'

Both Apple Inc. and Sony focused on innovation and cutting-edge technology and their products are always priced higher than their competitors. Everyone does not buy their products, but there are many customers who buy nothing but the best and an Apple or Sony product fits their bill. Likewise, a leader who promotes excellence cannot be followed by those who are below average performers or mediocre. And those who wish to garner the support of masses must not focus on excellence and discrimination, but talk of equality and justice.

All leaders must position themselves uniquely so that they become synonymous with the values they represent as a brand.

4. EFFECTIVE BRAND MANAGEMENT BUILDS REPUTATION

Once a leader is able to build a brand, he must make all efforts to maintain it. The brand of a leader is his reputation. This reputation can last only if it is genuine and is built on the edifice of strong character.

DL Moody, an American evangelist, who founded the Moody Church, Northfield School and the Moody Bible Institute said, 'If I take care of my character, my reputation will take care of itself.'

Forbes, in partnership with Burson-Marsteller, Penn Schoen Berland and Landor, conducted an exclusive, quantitative online survey in August 2011 to measure consumer perceptions of 100 top brands. The consumers were asked to rank the brands using a numeric scale of one to nine, based on twelve attributes:

1. Honest and trustworthy
2. Ethical leadership
3. Maintains high standards of quality in its products and services
4. Invests in innovative ideas and research
5. Upholds transparent communication practices
6. Invests in its customers
7. Dedicated to making communities a better place
8. Positively impacts the everyday lives of its customers
9. Leverages business success and expertise to make a positive contribution to society
10. Cares about the issues that matter to consumers
11. Understands and addresses the unique needs of consumers
12. Genuinely wants to make a difference in the world

Based on the survey, Johnson & Johnson became the number one brand.

What is true for a corporation is also true for a leader. Only if leaders try to perform consistently well in all of the above parameters, can they continue to enjoy a great brand image as leader. A single mistake can finish off their reputation, which may have been acquired over years.

Those who don't compromise their values and pay every price to uphold their brand, acquire a unique charisma and become the greatest leaders.

5

Aura of Charisma

Charisma is a sparkle in people that money can't buy. It's an invisible energy with visible effects.

—Marianne Williamson

Leadership, we have seen, is so much about personalities. Charisma is what adds to the personality. So a leader with charisma can be a great leader.

What is charisma? Charisma is defined as a rare personal quality attributed to leaders who arouse fervent popular devotion and enthusiasm. It refers to the personal magnetism or charm.

The word charisma is derived from the Greek word *kharisma*, meaning 'divine favour'. The ancient Greeks applied personality charisma to their gods. For example, they attributed charm, beauty, nature, human creativity or fertility to goddesses they called *Charites*.

Charisma is thus believed to be a divine attribute, which becomes a part of men, when they are blessed by God. When a person attempts to fulfil divine aspiration by sacrificing his selfish interest, he acquires charisma which the Almighty gifts to him to perform his function. It is this power that makes a person extraordinary and gives him power to perform a task which others consider impossible.

Interestingly, the charismatic leader rarely possesses a personality that is considered to be attractive. That is why, charisma is quite mysterious. Unlike models whose beauty and charm is visible and evident to all, the charm of a leader is quite mysterious. Charles de Gaulle, a French general and statesman who led the Free French Forces during WWII explained the importance of mystery in power. He said:

> There can be no power without mystery. There must always be a 'something' which others can't altogether fathom, which puzzles them, stirs them and rivets their attention...nothing more enhances authority than silence. It is the crowning virtue of the strong, the refuge of the weak, the modesty of the proud, the pride of the humble, the prudence of the wise and the sense of fools.

A leader seeks to build an emotional connect. So they develop a charisma by creating an air of invincibility and divinity around them. They become so extraordinary that people start believing that they can do anything. Their achievement in one field gets diffused into every field and they become charismatic, acquiring the quality of God.

Acquiring Charisma

Charisma is but a matter of belief. When followers believe that a leader has some extraordinary quality which is beyond their comprehension, they worship the person as a god. As long as the followers believe, the leader remains charismatic.

Just like beauty lies in the eyes of the beholder, charisma lies in the heart of the followers.

In order to understand charisma, we have to understand Divinity. There is none who has seen God, yet more than 90 per cent of the people in the world believe in God. They believe in scriptures, idols, saints, temples and churches and in priests and bishops.

Do any of the believers want proof of God?

There are so many scientists and scholars who have produced thousands of evidences that God does not exist, yet that does not deter billions from still believing. In fact, as more arguments advance for the nonexistence of God, the deeper may become their faith. Arguments can hardly change people, since for most arguments, there exists an equal and opposite counter argument. Consider the story often told by Shri Ramakrishna Paramhamsa,

> The master said, 'Everything that exists is God.' A pupil understood it literally, but not in the true spirit. While he was passing through a street, he met an elephant. The rider—*mahout*, shouted aloud from the elephant's back, his high place, 'Move away, move away!'
>
> The pupil argued in his mind, 'Why should I move away? I am God, and so is the elephant. What fear has God of Himself?' Thinking thus, he did not move.
>
> The elephant then took him up by his trunk, and threw him aside. He was severely hurt and going back to his master, he related the whole sorry adventure.
>
> The master said, 'All right, you are God. The elephant is God also, but God in the shape of the elephant-rider was also warning you. Why did you not pay heed to his warnings?'

Proofs are sought only by non-believers and atheists. For a believer, his heart is proof enough. When the master is saying something, it must be true.

Even those who are believers, tend to believe only in their own God, disbelieving the rest. In the words of Richard Dawkins, 'We are all atheists about most of the gods that humanity has ever believed in. Some of us just go one god further.'

Charisma is about Miracles and Hope

We believe in God because we want miracles. Those who never need miracles may disbelieve in God. We wish for a saviour who can protect us and help us tide over problems that seem insurmountable.

Hence, when we come across a person who has proven to be capable of solving difficult problems in life, we consider the person divine too, and believe in his charisma. Charisma is thus connected with hope, which implies seeking fulfilment not by our own effort, but by some miracle of God. One who promises us such fulfilment becomes a charismatic leader, as he seems to have been sent by God to fulfil our desires. A charismatic leader is thus full of divine qualities.

The Qualities of a Charismatic Leader

1. **Confidence:** A charismatic leader is full of confidence. His confidence is supported by his success. He never gives the impression that there is anything in the world that he cannot do. That provides proof of his boundless capability bordering on divine power. His confidence is like an epidemic, which soon spreads to everyone.
2. **Uniqueness:** A charismatic person is unique. He copies no one. He has no hero, but his own self. He is not implementing anyone's vision or ideology as he creates his own ideology and then converts it into reality.
3. **Passion:** A charismatic leader is full of energy and passion. He seems tireless and cheerful. He is in a hurry to complete his task at the earliest. His passion fills his supporters with tremendous passion and has the multiplier effect.
4. **Focus:** You become charismatic when you have focus. When you do not know where to go, any road is okay. But a

charismatic leader is focused and has the road map. He does not change his goalpost to suit the needs of time. All his energy is directed at arriving and completing the task. Hence, people believe him. If he has promised, he delivers.

5. **Divine Qualities:** A leader becomes charismatic by imbibing the attributes of God in him. He seems to be selfless, incorruptible, honest, powerful, knowledgeable, wise and working for the sake of the world only. These qualities are the attributes of God and that make him divine. He seems to be above all criticism, personal comfort and achievement but focused on the interest of only others.

6. **Clairvoyant:** A charismatic leader declares his plans in advance to the public thereby arousing anticipation in the minds and hearts of people. Thereafter, he accomplishes his goal as promised. Thus, a leader displays clairvoyance and foresight, which gradually make the people trust his words and believe his promises.

A leader must develop charisma consciously, as his followers follow him like they follow God, and with this joint effort nothing should be impossible.

Creating an Aura Calls for Much Effort

Few are born with charisma. It is mostly acquired by systematic planning and effort and seeking the help of an advisor who creates an aura. The best way to understand charisma is to understand how movies create heroes. If you get to meet such a hero in real life, you may find him very ordinary. There are many more handsome and charming people around, yet the hero is different as he seems to be free of any defect and is full of all virtues.

The charismatic personality of a leader is the collective effort of a large number of people who remain in the background, but are responsible for the aura of the leader. It is, therefore, necessary to have the right advisor for a leader. Chandragupta Maurya could not have become the king but for the advice of Chanakya. Pandavas may not have won the battle, but for the advice of Lord Krishna who did not fight himself. Even Lord Rama could not have killed Ravana without the counsel of wise Jamavanta and the advice given by Vibhishana, the brother of Ravana who had defected. He who has wrong advisor perishes while he who has the best advisor emerges as the most charismatic leader.

A leader must identify people with different talents and use their talent to supplement his own weaknesses. A charismatic leader can't afford to have a single defect. As Indian saint and poet, Tulsidas said, 'The all-powerful person can have no defect'—*Samrath ko nahi dosh gosai*.

In other words, if you have any visible defects, you cannot be charismatic.

God is perfect and so is a charismatic leader.

PART V

DEVELOPING LEADERSHIP

1

A Powerful Idea

A man may die, nations may rise and fall, but an idea lives on.
—John F Kennedy

Leaders are men of ideas. They change the status quo of the world. Just imagine how man was living thousands of years back. There was hardly any difference between him and other animals. Yet, a few men with great ideas transformed the world.

There has never been a dearth of ideas, but there are few who really believe in an idea so much that they give up everything for it and work at transforming the idea into reality. When an idea is transformed into reality, an ordinary person gets transformed into a leader. Swami Vivekananda, a man of action and one of the foremost spiritual leaders of India, stated very clearly, 'Take up one idea. Make that one idea your life—think of it, dream of it, live on that idea. Let the brain, muscles, nerves, every part of your body, be full of that idea and just leave every other idea alone. This is the way to success.'

A leader may not be a great thinker. He may not have an idea of his own, but he knows how to convert an idea into reality. A leader is the bridge between thoughts and reality. A leader is a practical person who has a deep understanding of people, he knows what they want and how their aspirations can be fulfilled.

Ideas Drive Leaders to Their Goals

Even the greatest idea is not new. Most ideas have existed in this world since time immemorial, but it requires the genius of a leader to use the idea to achieve the desired objectives.

Take the concept of truth and non-violence, which formed the core of Gandhi's freedom movement in India against the British. He implemented this idea when everyone in the world was talking about wars. His career in India virtually began with the start of the WWI and ended with the end of WWII. While the world was talking about war, he was talking about peace and getting increasingly popular, both in India and abroad. Yet, there was nothing new in his idea as he has honestly admitted, 'I have nothing new to teach the world. Truth and non-violence are as old as the hills. All I have done is to try experiments in both on as vast a scale as I could.'

Thousands of years back, Buddha preached non-violence in the East, while Jesus preached it in the West. Yet, the methods adopted by Gandhi to implement the idea were not based on either Jesus or Buddha, but actually on the principles enumerated in Leo Tolstoy's book, *The Kingdom of God is Within You*. The book was rejected and banned in Russia and Leo Tolstoy was excommunicated, but Gandhi used the idea successfully to unite hundreds of millions of Indians.

Gandhi wrote in his autobiography:

> Tolstoy's *The Kingdom of God is Within You*, left an abiding impression on me. Before the independent thinking, profound morality and the truthfulness of this book, all the books given to me by Mr Coates seemed to pale into insignificance.... I made

too an intensive study of Tolstoy's books. *The Gospels in Brief*, *What to Do?* and other books.... I began to realise more and more the infinite possibilities of universal love.

It is, however, incorrect to infer that there was something great in the idea of non-violence. If that would have been so, every leader would have followed non-violence. In fact, the opposite of a great idea is often an equally great idea. There are great leaders who believed that violence is the right way and they achieved success through violence. Take the case of Mao Tse-tung, who transformed China and made it one of the most powerful and developed countries of the world. He said, 'A revolution is not a dinner party or writing an essay or painting a picture or doing embroidery; it can't be so refined, so leisurely and gentle, so temperate, kind, courteous, restrained and magnanimous. A revolution is an insurrection, an act of violence by which one class overthrows another.'

If Gandhi believed in loving even enemies and criticised the policy of 'an eye for an eye', Mao proclaimed, 'War can only be abolished through war, and in order to get rid of the gun, it is necessary to take up the gun.'

Converting Ideas to Benefit Society

Societies are transformed by leaders by converting an idea into reality. Stalin and Lenin converted the idea of socialism propounded by Karl Marx into reality. Mao implemented the same with some modification in China—which is known now as Maoism. Even Hitler, who is considered to be one of the most unethical leaders of the twentieth century, achieved all success based on the idea of evolution given by Darwin. He convinced the German people that they have the right to rule the world by virtue of being the superior race. He said in his autobiography, *Mein Kampf*:

> For the establishment of superior type of civilisation, the members of inferior races formed one of the most essential prerequisites.

They alone could supply the lack of mechanical means, without which no progress is possible. It is certain that the first stages of human civilisation were not based on the use of tame animals as on the employment of human beings who were members of inferior races.... Only after subjugated races were employed as slaves, was a similar fate allotted to animals, and not vice versa, as some people would have us believe. At first it was the conquered enemy who had to draw the plough as only afterwards did the ox and horse take his place.

He described the Aryans as the most superior race, who hence have the right to rule the world. He went on to say:

All the human culture, all the results of art, science and technology...are almost exclusively the creative product of the Aryan.... He is the Prometheus of mankind from whose bright forehead the divine spark of genius has sprung at all times, forever kindling anew the fire of knowledge which illumined the night of silent mysteries and thus caused man to climb the path to mastery over the other beings of this earth.

One of the greatest US presidents, Abraham Lincoln too was an idealist; his ideals were based on The Bible. He believed in the principle of equality of races and risked a Civil War to uphold his principles. He said, 'This is a world of compensations, and he who would be no slave, must consent to have no slave. Those who deny freedom to others deserve it not for themselves, and under a just God, can't long retain it.'

Not only political leaders, industry leaders too are usually men of ideas. Bill Gates too, who created the greatest software company of the world—Microsoft Corporation, is motivated by ideas. He says, 'I'm a great believer that any tool that enhances communication has profound effects in terms of how people can learn from each other, and how they can achieve the kind of freedoms that they're interested in.'

Pursuing his idea, Gates offered the world the Windows operating system, which changed personal computing forever.

A leader is born when he becomes a living epitome of an idea. He gives life to an idea by giving it his blood, sweat and creativity. Steve Jobs, one of the greatest entrepreneurs and innovators of modern time rightly said, 'Innovation distinguishes between a leader and a follower.'

The Birth of a Leader

If you wish to be a leader, it helps if you have an idea that can change the world. Having compassion for the underprivileged can be one ideal, while promoting excellence by competition can be another. You can choose any great idea, which fills your mind and heart and work to convert it into reality by improvising it with your creative energy. Older ideas need to be modified, polished and recreated for the modern times.

Once you have an idea and a burning desire, you find creative means to achieve your goal. Steve Jobs states:

> Creativity is just connecting things. When you ask creative people how they did something, they feel a little guilty because they didn't really do it, they just saw something. It seemed obvious to them after a while. That's because they were able to connect experiences they've had and synthesise new things.

A leader creates a new idea by assimilating many old ideas like an architect uses existing bricks and mortars to make a new building. For his innovative approach, the leader gets due credit.

Every idea is met with resistance initially as people usually fail to recognise how powerful it is. 'First they ignore you, then they laugh at you, then they fight you, then you win,' said Mahatma Gandhi, whose idea of truth and non-violence was much ridiculed by the people of his time. Yet, he won due to his faith in the idea. He first used the idea on himself and then advised others to follow suit. As he walked his talk on this most difficult path, others joined him and a great leader was born.

There is no dearth of ideas in this world. Every person has an idea that can change the world but they do not want to implement it on themselves because they are not quite ready to accept that it might work. Here's an example of such hesitation.

> A man accidently fell off a cliff. As he was falling, he grabbed the branch of a tree sticking out from the side of the cliff, and looked down 300 feet to the ground below, and then looked up and said, 'Lord, if there's anyone up there, give me faith. Tell me what to do.'
>
> And a voice from the heavens said, 'If you have faith, let go.'
>
> He looked down at the ground and then took look up again and said, 'Is there anyone else up there?'

Mahatma Gandhi had said, 'Be the change you wish to see in the world.' But most people throw new ideas only to prove a point or for the sake of discussion only. The more outlandish the idea, the greater attention it gets. As the Indian saint and poet Tulsidas wisely said, 'There are many experts to advise others.'

No wonder we hardly take an idea seriously when it is coming from a person who himself does not follow his ideas and has thus no experience in successfully implementing it.

A leader is one who applies an idea to the self. He becomes the change agent. If your idea is really great, there is no reason not to buy the idea yourself and implement it in your own life. While there is no dearth of people talking about the ideas of equality and justice only to garner advantage for themselves by trying to be equal to those who are better than them, Gandhi implemented equality in the true spirit when he worked as a scavenger. The following incident from his life illustrates this:

In the meantime, Gandhiji asked the scavengers not to do any work for a few days. The high-caste boys could never think of doing the work of untouchable scavengers. Life in the school became almost impossible with the odour of night-soil. Then Gandhiji himself carried the pots on his own head...and buried the contents underground. This super-human act was contagious. Soon the boys of the highest castes and rich families were vying with one another to have the honour of doing the work of the outcaste scavengers.

An idea is just an ideal till a leader breathes life into it. When a person follows an idea, he becomes the living force behind the idea, subordinates himself and serves the idea like it is God. Some people believe that God itself is an idea that changed the human race. The greatness of a person lies in the ideal for which he is working.

A man came across three masons who were working at chipping chunks of granite from large blocks. The first seemed unhappy with his job and as he chipped, he glanced frequently at his watch. When the man asked him what he was doing, he responded rather curtly, 'I'm hammering this stupid rock, and I can't wait till five, when I can go home.'

The second mason, seemingly more interested in his work, was hammering diligently. When asked what it was that he was doing, answered, 'Well, I'm moulding this block of rock so that it can be used with others to construct a wall. It's not bad work, but I'll sure be glad when it's done.'

The third mason was hammering at his block fervently, taking time to stand back and admire his work. He chipped off small pieces until he was satisfied that it was the best he could do. When he was questioned about his work, he stopped, gazed skyward and proudly proclaimed, 'I...am building a cathedral!'

Three men; three different attitudes; all doing the same job.

And when you fight for an idea that you consider sacrosanct, you cannot afford to lose. If Gandhi would have failed, it would have been the defeat of the idea of non-violence. When masses accept your idea as their own, you become a leader. By succeeding in his non-violence movement, Gandhi gave the world a new idea. Non-violence became a respectable and practical ideal. It was reborn in the modern world and made the world a little more peaceful and compassionate.

2

Get a Grip on the Complete Reality

Never mistake knowledge for wisdom. One helps you make a living; the other helps you make a life.

—Sandra Carey

To make ideas work, you need knowledge. Accurate knowledge of reality is extremely important for success in any job. If you are not well-prepared and lack training, you may struggle hard but are unlikely to succeed. Just like you can't cut the tree with a blunt axe, you can't achieve your goals without accurate knowledge. Hence, Abraham Lincoln said, 'If I had six hours to chop down a tree, I'd spend the first four hours sharpening the axe.' Most of us, however, jump to conclusions even when our knowledge is incomplete.

> 'My grandfather knew exactly the date and time of his death,' said John to his friend Peter.
>
> Peter: 'Wow! He was surely an evolved soul. I am sure he must have done many noble deeds in his life. How did he come to know of his death so accurately?'

'He was told by the judge,' said Peter.

The importance of knowledge has been stated by Sun Tzu in *The Art of War*, 'If you know the enemy and know yourself, you need not fear the result of a hundred battles. If you know yourself but not the enemy, for every victory gained you will also suffer a defeat. If you know neither the enemy nor yourself, you will succumb in every battle.'

Intelligence can help a person to accurately map the competition so that when he is actually fighting, he is prepared to counter all the moves of his opponents, and also has some secret plans of which the enemy has no clue.

Thus, every leader must gain true knowledge before he goes to the battlefield. True knowledge includes:

- Knowing the self
- Knowing others
- Knowledge of strategies

Once in the battlefield, he uses the option best suited for the situation, based on his prior knowledge and rehearsed moves.

1. Knowing the Self

When we intend to sell any product, we must know all its strengths and weaknesses. Knowledge of its negatives helps us defend our product and awareness of positives ensures that we convince the buyer of its value. How well the salesman knows his product determines the quantum of his sales.

A leader too must know himself well in order to pitch himself optimally before his followers. He must know his strengths and weaknesses. Quite often we like to see only our positive side and ignore the negatives. Sometimes, we even try to justify the negatives to keep our morale and self-esteem high. But it is important to introspect and analyse our likes and dislikes.

We also need to know ourselves from the perspective of others—our friends, rivals and even neutral people. Our friends can list our strengths while our enemies point out our weaknesses. It is foolish to expect praise from your enemies.

> 'What was wrong with you tonight? Your playing lacked fire,' a friend said to the famous pianist, Leopold Godowasy, as he was leaving the concert hall after the recital.
>
> 'I know,' agreed Godowasky. 'It wasn't my best performance.'
>
> Just then one of his greatest rivals rushed up to him and shook hands, crying excitingly. 'Leopold, you were wonderful tonight, I have never heard you play better!'
>
> When the other pianist had gone, Godowsky frowned and muttered, 'I didn't realise I was that bad.'

It is, therefore, important to listen to criticism objectively, as there is always some truth in all criticisms. The critics are the best people who acquaint us with our weaknesses. And for a complete picture, we must also hear the views of independent people.

2. Knowing Others

Knowing the self is intimately connected with knowing others. The world is like a mirror. Just like we can't see our face but for the mirror, we can't know ourselves without knowing the world. Hence, the true knowledge of the world comes by knowing the self and we know ourselves well when we know the world accurately. Most people fail to know the world primarily because they fail to know their own selves. It is due to their ignorance that most people are always criticising the world. Dale Carnegie said, 'Instead of condemning people, let's try to understand them. Let's try to figure out why they do what they do. That's a lot more profitable and intriguing than criticism, and it breeds sympathy, tolerance and kindness. To know all is to forgive all.'

True knowledge is the foundation of all love and understanding. If we know a person intimately, we touch his soul through ours, and get to know everything about that person. Newspaper columnist, Nixon Waterman explains this so well:

> If I knew you and you knew me,
> If both of us could clearly see,
> And with an inner sight divine,
> The meaning of your heart and mine,
> I'm sure that we would differ less,
> And clasp our hands in friendliness,
> Our thoughts would pleasantly agree,
> If I knew you and you knew me.

3. Knowledge of Strategies

Just like a general must master different strategies for the battlefield, a leader must also be an expert strategist to overcome his rivals. You need not rediscover the wheel, but learn from the experience of others.

For Example, *Art of War* lists following strategies for the warrior:

> It is the rule in war, if ten times the enemy's strength, surround them; if five times, attack them; if double, be able to divide them; if equal, engage them; if fewer, be able to evade them; if weaker, be able to avoid them.... If your enemy is secure at all points, be prepared for him. If he is in superior strength, evade him. If your opponent is temperamental, seek to irritate him. Pretend to be weak, that he may grow arrogant. If he is taking his ease, give him no rest. If his forces are united, separate them. If sovereign and subject are in accord, put division between them. Attack him where he is unprepared, appear where you are not expected.

Only when you know the different options, can you take the right decision, at the right time. However, excess of knowledge is as dangerous as the lack of knowledge. That's because knowledge is food for thought. If consumed less, it starves the mind and when in excess, it confuses the mind, as is evident from this Aesop's fable:

> A fox was boasting to a cat of clever devices for escaping its enemies.
>
> 'I have a whole bag of tricks,' he said, 'which contains a hundred ways of escaping my enemies.'
>
> 'I have only one,' said the cat, 'but I can generally manage with that.'
>
> Just at that moment they heard the cry of a pack of hounds coming towards them, and the cat immediately scampered up a tree and hid herself in the boughs.
>
> 'This is my plan,' said the cat. 'What are you going to do?'
>
> The fox thought first of one way, then of another and while he was thus debating, the hounds came nearer and nearer and at last, the fox in his confusion was caught up by the hounds and soon killed by the huntsmen.

Arrive at a Decision

You need not have complete knowledge of the world, no one can. Consult experienced people before taking a decision. When people give their opinion freely and honestly, it ensures that all options have been considered and you are not caught unawares. However, once a decision is taken, stick to it. Once a leader accepts the decision, he must accept failures if any, while giving credit to all if it succeeds. In the words of Bill Gates, 'Don't make the same decision twice. Spend time and thought to make a solid decision the first time, so that you don't revisit the issue unnecessarily. If you're too willing to reopen issues, it interferes not only with your execution, but also with your motivation to make a decision in the first place. After all, why bother deciding an issue if it isn't really decided?'

Sharpen Your Axe

Even though there is no substitute for real life experience and knowledge acquired through it, wise people learn from the experience of others, and improvise knowledge to suit their needs. Mere bookish knowledge is of no value unless its fundamentals are understood properly. Only then can you convey the message to your followers. As Einstein said, 'If you can't explain it simply, you don't understand it well enough.'

The value of knowledge is in its application, which alone can provide benefit to the knower. Leaders thus not only strive to acquire knowledge but also apply it in real life and develop a true understanding of it.

Once his knowledge is accurate and the intellect knows how to put the right knowledge to use, there is nothing that a leader can't achieve.

3

Developing Imagination

Imagination is more important than knowledge. For knowledge is limited, whereas imagination embraces the entire world, stimulating progress, giving birth to evolution. It is, strictly speaking, a real factor in scientific research.

—Albert Einstein

We saw that a leader must try to know and understand the complete reality. A strong imagination can make this task easier. Einstein is considered to be one of the most innovative scientists. He never visited a lab or carried out experiments to discover the laws of nature. All his theories emerged from his mind, his only lab.

For an innovative person, the whole world is a book and every person is a chapter of the book. His mind creates a miniature world 'within' from where he discovers the solutions to life's problems. Solutions come in the form of intuition, just like the right method to solve a maths problem occurs to a student who has solved many similar problems. Einstein said, 'I believe in intuition and inspiration. At times, I feel certain I am right while not knowing the reason. When the eclipse of

1919 confirmed my intuition, I was not in the least surprised. In fact, I would have been astonished had it turned out otherwise.'

What was confirmed in 1919 by scientists was that bending of rays due to the forces of gravity, was predicted by Einstein in his General Theory of Relativity in 1916. All the great theories he discovered through his imagination were later proven by experiments.

Just as a scientist deciphers the laws of nature and a writer sees into the minds of his readers through his imagination—a leader too knows the world through his imagination. A politician can often gain incredible insight into the minds and desires of his supporters or opponents simply by looking at them. Lyndon Baines Johnson, former president of the United States once said, 'When you walked into a room and you can't tell who is for you and who is against you, you don't belong to politics.' Great leaders know more than what the mind, senses and intellect can deduct by logic and facts.

The Power of Imagination

Imagination allows you to form a picture in your mind of something that you have not seen or experienced. It is the ability to think of new thoughts, and that can tremendously help in problem-solving, something which every leader has to do, all the time.

This is how the girl in this story uses her innovative mind to settle her issues.

> Many years ago in a small village, a farmer had the misfortune of owing a large sum of money to a village moneylender. The moneylender, who was old and ugly, fancied the farmer's beautiful daughter. So he proposed a bargain. He said he would forgo the farmer's debt if he could marry his daughter. Both the farmer and his daughter were horrified by the proposal. So the cunning moneylender suggested that they let providence decide the matter.

He told them that he would put a black pebble and a white pebble into an empty money bag. Then the girl would have to pick one pebble from the bag.

1. If she picked the black pebble, she would become his wife and her father's debt would be forgiven.
2. If she picked the white pebble she need not marry him and her father's debt would still be forgiven.
3. But if she refused to pick a pebble, her father would be thrown into jail.

They were standing on a pebble-strewn path in the farmer's field. As they talked, the moneylender bent over to pick up two pebbles. When he picked them up, the sharp-eyed girl noticed that he had picked up two black pebbles to put into the bag.

He then asked the girl to pick a pebble from this bag. It was not feasible for the girl or her father to point out the fraud to the moneylender.

Now, imagine that you were standing in the field. What would you have done if you were the girl? If you had to advise her, what would you have told her?

Careful analysis would produce three possibilities:

1. The girl should refuse to take a pebble.
2. The girl should show that there were two black pebbles in the bag and expose the moneylender as a cheat.
3. The girl should pick a black pebble and sacrifice herself in order to save her father from his debt and imprisonment.

What do you think the girl did?

The girl put her hand into the bag and drew out a pebble. Without looking at it, she fumbled and let it fall onto the pebble-strewn path where it immediately got lost amongst all the other pebbles.

> 'Oh, how clumsy of me,' she said. 'But never mind, if you look into the bag for the one that is left, you will be able to tell which pebble I picked.'
>
> Since the remaining pebble was black, it had to be assumed that she had picked the white one. And since the moneylender dared not admit his dishonesty, the girl changed what seemed like an impossible situation, into an extremely advantageous one.

This is the power of imagination. It rescued the girl and her father from the clutches of the moneylender. If most of us are unable to get over our problems, it is mainly because we lack imagination. We try to deal with our issues in the old and familiar way, and we fail because no two problems are alike, and what worked earlier may not work again in real life. Einstein was right when he said, 'We can't solve our problems with the same level of thinking that created them.'

Need to Imagine Correctly

We all imagine things in our mind, in the daylight as well as in our dreams. However, all imaginations are not accurate. Most of our problems are due to our lack of ability to imagine correctly.

Often our imagination is not correct since we lack the correct knowledge of the world. Our imagination is also tainted by our wishful thinking, emotions and our hatred or love. We mix our desires with the knowledge of reality. It is this difference in imagination that the same world is heaven for some, while hell for others. So a leader has to imagine right, unlike the patient in this story.

> A hypochondriac man went to the doctor and said, 'Doctor! I am very tense. I am sure that I have got liver disease.'
>
> The doctor said, 'That is absolutely ridiculous. There is no discomfort of any kind in case of liver disease.'
>
> 'Exactly!' said the man. 'These are my precise symptoms.'

For most of us, the world seen by us is not as it is, but as we are. So we imagine the reality as not what it truly is, but what it should be according to our desires. When depressed, we see it at its worst. Then if our boss points out a minor error in our work, we imagine that he is quite upset and angry and will surely damage our career. So we turn too conscious. At this point, if we catch our colleagues or subordinates chatting, we imagine that they are conspiring against us.

Similarly, when we are optimistic, in love or in a good mood, we see a very positive picture of the world. Everything looks beautiful and benevolent. So even if the boss seems upset, we believe he may be having some personal problem. And if we catch others chatting, we imagine they are praising us.

When we are not balanced, we suffer. An optimist suffers when he faces reality, while the pessimist suffers all the time due to his fear and distrust.

Only when our imagination is correct do we succeed and feel happy from the beginning till the end. That's how a leader should imagine. For such imagination, he must be free from personal bias, love or hatred, optimism or pessimism.

Imagination Gives Birth to Innovation

Imagination is the mother of innovation. It is said that everything is created twice in the world. Before anything is created in the material world, the same is created in our imagination.

The world is constantly in a state of flux. We change every moment, so do everyone else and so does the reality.

Lal Bahadur Shastri, the former prime minister of India said rightly, 'A leader, generally, if he is really a leader, does not walk on beaten tracks, because political field situations change, men change, conditions change and environment changes, and a real leader must match his policies to the changing conditions.' It is impossible to succeed by imitating any other successful person as narrated by this story written thousands of years ago in *Aesop's Fables*.

> A farmer one day came to the stables to see to his beasts of burden: Among them was his favourite ass that was always well-fed and often carried him. With the farmer came his lapdog that danced about and licked his hand and frisked about as happy as it could be. The farmer felt in his pocket, gave the lapdog food and sat down while he gave his orders to his servants. The lapdog jumped into his master's lap, and lay there blinking while the farmer stroked his ears.
>
> The ass, seeing this, broke loose from his halter and commenced prancing about in imitation of the lapdog. The farmer could not hold his sides with laughter, so the ass went up to him, and putting his feet upon the farmer's shoulder attempted to climb into his lap. The farmer's servants rushed up with sticks and pitchforks and soon taught the ass a lesson: Never imitate anyone.

If imitation would have been the recipe for success, every successful leader in history would have numerous clones today. In reality, we see none, as every successful leader succeeds in his own unique way.

Yet, there is nothing new in this world. Every new thing is created from what already exists. So a creative leader is one who is in touch with reality and through his imagination develops an accurate model of the world, just like engineers build an accurate model of an airplane before the actual plane is manufactured.

An innovative person simulates the outcome of an action in his mental laboratory, testing different ideas and their effect on this imaginary world where he intends to apply his idea. Thus, he is able to select the idea or 'a fusion of ideas', which would work best to yield the desired result. Thus, the leader brings a new idea into the world. His greatest challenge is to convince other people of his idea, which worked best in his mental world. So the first thing that a leader does is to sell them his belief about his new idea. People do not believe as such in the idea of the leader, but they believe in their leader and hence, in his idea.

People buy the leader before buying the idea.

However, in order to get people to fully accept the idea of the leader, it needs to be converted into reality. Imagination thus becomes knowledge only when it is materialised by the reality of a leader's actions.

4

Taking Initiatives

Initiative is doing the right thing without being told.

–Victor Hugo

A great leader takes the initiative with full faith in his heart to accomplish the mission. Leadership is an act driven by initiative. 'Without initiative,' said Bo Bennett, a successful online entrepreneur, 'leaders are simply workers in leadership positions.'

No one can force a person to become a leader even if they are in the top position. You may not be able to take an initiative even as the head of a team. Johann Wolfgang von Goethe, a German writer and politician said aptly, 'Thinking is easy, acting is difficult, and to put one's thoughts into action is the most difficult thing in the world.'

It is this drive to convert thoughts into action that distinguishes a leader from the rest. In any organisation, people can be divided into the following four categories.

1. **Leader:** They are the people who do the right things without being told to do so.

2. **Follower:** They do the right things when told.
3. **Shirker:** They try to avoid work as they don't like work.
4. **Resister:** They are obstinate and oppose any change in the organisation.

There is always a shortage of leaders in any organisation. They are always in demand and they are rewarded the best.

The followers are leaders in making. They are the managers who implement the vision of a leader. Working closely with the leader, they gradually develop the vision of the leader.

Shirkers can be motivated to work provided they are rewarded, appreciated for their good work and punished for not doing the work. However, they consume a lot of the management's energy, which might not be worth it beyond a point.

The resisters are the negative elements in the organisation who neither work themselves, nor let others work. An organisation is better off without them.

Taking Initiative

We all dream of a beautiful future. It is this hope of a better future that sustains our life and fills it with joy. Yet, when the future becomes the present, we fail to enjoy it as it does not fit into our dream. Peter F Drucker said, 'The best way to predict your future is to create it.' And you create your future by initiative.

How to take initiative?

It is not difficult to take initiatives. People can usually see what is required to be done to make the world a better place for us and our future generations. Yet, whenever we wish to do something new, we fear failure and criticism. It is not easy to overcome it, as often our first response is 'It couldn't be done' as Edgar Guest asserts in this beautiful poem:

> Somebody said that it couldn't be done
> But he with a chuckle replied
> That 'maybe it couldn't,' but he would be one
> Who wouldn't say so till he tried.
> So he buckled right in with the trace of a grin
> On his face, if he worried he hid it.
> He started to sing as he tackled the thing
> That couldn't be done, and he did it.

Initiative is required in everything, as everything can be improved with effort and action. But if you try improving everything at the same time, you may fail due to lack of focus and dissipation of energy in different directions. Even if you succeed in one, the list of failures would be much longer and you should not be surprised when people talk mainly about your failed initiatives than your success.

A good leader must create an aura of invincibility around him. If he starts, he must finish. Losing is not an option. Even if he loses, that must only be an exception and the loss should be partial, so that the leader can, at least, claim partial success.

While choosing the initiatives to be taken, take following factors into consideration:

1. Resolve Urgent Problems Immediately

When you are suffering from fever or headache, the first need even before curing the disease is to take care of the symptoms. You immediately take medicines that give you relief from pain and fever.

Leaders must thus focus their attention on solving problems which are urgent and leave those that are irritating but unlikely to trouble the organisation for long. If you treat every problem as urgent, you are likely to spend all your time firefighting only. However, when an issue gets solved, there must be proactive measures to ensure it is not repeated.

This is done by going to the root of the problem and providing lasting solutions by taking necessary initiatives.

2. Focus on Problems with Highest Impact

Once the urgency is resolved and life is back on track, leaders must identify problem areas, which can create maximum impact with minimum effort. They must invest their time and energy in cases where the rate of return is high. When a major issue is resolved, it improves the performance of the organisation and boosts the confidence of the employees. Leaders do not dwell on petty issues whose impact is negligible.

> A certain rich man in Springfield, Illinois, sued a poor attorney for $2.50, and Lincoln was asked to prosecute the case.
>
> Lincoln urged the creditor to let the matter drop adding, 'You can make nothing out of him, and it will cost you a good deal more than the debt to bring suit.'
>
> The creditor was still determined to have his way, and threatened to seek some other attorney. Lincoln then said, 'Well, if you are determined that suit should be brought, I will bring it but my charge will be $10.'
>
> The money was paid to him, and peremptory orders were given that the suit be brought that day. After the client's departure, Lincoln went out of the office, returning in about an hour with an amused look on his face.
>
> Asked what pleased him, he replied, 'I brought the suit against, and then hunted him up, told him what I had done, handed him half of the $10, and we went over to the squire's office. He confessed, judgment was passed and bill paid.'
>
> Lincoln added that he didn't see any other way to make things satisfactory for his client as well as the other.

There are some problems whose solutions may be simple but their impact may be very high. These are often called the broken window problems, which was first introduced by social scientists, James Q Wilson and George L Kelling, in an article titled 'Broken Windows' which appeared in the March 1982 edition of *The Atlantic Monthly*. The title comes from the following example:

> Consider a building with a few broken windows. If the windows are not repaired, the tendency is for vandals to break a few more windows. Eventually, they may even break into the building, and if it's unoccupied, perhaps become squatters or light fires inside. Or consider a pavement. Some litter accumulates. Soon, more litter accumulates. Eventually, people even start leaving bags of refuse from take-out restaurants there or even break into cars. These small matters can make a great change in future. Just like a small scratch can spoil the beauty of a car, these small irritant problems can spoil the image of the organisation.

Once the problem of greatest impact is tackled, the next best can be picked. As a leader, you must focus on issues that greatly affect performance, while the routine problems can be resolved by the managers.

3. Develop Excellence in Your Organisation

A leader must take action not only to resolve issues, but to also foster excellence in the organisation. He must take up initiatives which can take the organisation to the next level. There is need to move from individual solutions to system-based solutions. Only when the leader rises to the next level can he solve problems of the lower level. In the words of Peter Drucker:

The effective executive makes sure that the job is well-designed. And if experience tells him otherwise, he does not hunt for genius to do the impossible. He redesigns the job. He knows that the test of organisation is not genius. It is its capacity to make common people achieve uncommon performance.

Leaders take initiative and create the future. They take care of the future by investing part of their present for the future, and reap success and peace later.

5

Developing Courage

Courage is the most important of all the virtues because without courage, you can't practice any other virtue consistently.

–Maya Angelou

A leader, we know, must strategise, draw upon his imagination, take up initiatives, mobilise support and act. But all this requires courage. It is easy to think and plan, but extremely difficult to execute as 'every action creates an equal and opposite reaction'. This is Newton's Third Law of Motion, but it is equally valid for all types of actions. Let us recapitulate the three laws of motion given by Newton, which are equally valid for human life.

- **First Law-The Law of Inertia:** An object at rest will remain at rest and object in motion continues to be in motion unless acted on by force.
- **Second Law-The Law of Acceleration:** The acceleration—the rate of change of speed of an object is directly proportional to the force applied on it.

- **Third Law-The Law of Reaction:** For every action, there is an equal and opposite reaction.

When we use the First Law in human endeavour, we find that if no initiative is taken by anyone, the world would stay as it is. The world is beset with issues like poverty, injustice, inequality, pain and suffering, and you wish to change them. But the same is not possible unless you stand up to oppose the forces that are responsible for these problems. There is a need to take a concrete stand against prevailing issues.

The Second Law stipulates that if the force is more, change is more rapid and the desired results shall be visible sooner. Hence, leaders should take the support of their followers, so that they can multiply the force and achieve faster results. Individual effort, we know can produce limited results over time, whereas the force of a movement can usher in big changes immediately.

Now, the Third Law states that whenever you wish to change the world by applying force, you are bound to face equal and opposite reaction. That is, for every blow you give to this world, you have to suffer an equally harsh one. If people avoid changing the status quo and prefer to live peacefully, it is probably because they lack courage to face what comes in return. But leaders need to take up initiatives and suffer blows in its wake to get result.

As American poet and essayist, Ralph Waldo Emerson said, 'Whatever course you decide upon, there is always someone to tell you that you are wrong. There are always difficulties arising which tempt you to believe that your critics are right. To map out a course of action and follow it to an end requires courage.'

You may have tremendous initiative, enthusiasm and energy and you may also be quite creative, but everything is useless unless you convert your thoughts into action—which needs courage. Novelist CS Lewis emphatically pronounced, 'Courage is not simply one of the virtues, but the form of every virtue at the testing point. Every good thought is good for nothing unless you have courage of conviction which overpowers the fear of defeat.'

The Valour of the Courageous

When Arjuna was confronted in the battlefield by the Kaurava forces, he got frightened. On the opposite side were some of the greatest warriors of the time like Bhishma, Drona and Karna, whom Arjuna had never battled. He, however, did not directly express his fear of defeat, instead took refuge in sentiments, speaking of love, compassion and relationship, and claiming that he could not fight against his relatives, elders and guru. Lord Krishna recognised Arjuna's fear and convinced him to fight, saying, 'If you are killed, you win heaven; if you triumph, you enjoy the earth. Therefore, Arjuna, stand up and resolve to fight the battle.'

Developing Courage

Mere knowledge and good intentions are no good unless these are used to produce the desired result. For that you need courage, and courage is not something inborn, but has to be developed.

The good news is that we can all develop courage. When a person joins the army, he is like any other young man. However, within a few of months, the cadet develops tremendous courage and is prepared to lay his life for the country. The virtue of courage is developed in him bit-by-bit, just like we build muscles gradually when training in the gym. By putting ourselves in the adverse situation with determination to become victorious, we develop courage. But then as the following story depicts, like any other developed trait, there is always a limit to the courage of a person.

> Once, a captain on his ship was disturbed by his assistant screaming, 'Sir! Sir! There are five enemy ships on the horizon.'

The captain tells the man, 'Get my red coat and prepare for battle!'

The assistant ran without a question to get the captain's red coat and prepared for battle. After their victory, the assistant asked the captain why he wanted his red coat. The captain told the assistant 'If I was shot, you would not be able to tell I'm bleeding, and you would keep fighting.'

The assistant thought this was a great idea. The next day, the assistant came to the captain, 'Sir! Sir! There are twenty enemy ships on the horizon!'

The captain was stunned. He looked at the assistant and told him, 'Get me my brown pants!'

The source of courage is the conviction that there is something more important than comfort, fear of failure or even our own life. An ordinary person develops tremendous courage when his loved one is attacked. Parents can give up their lives to save their children. If we lack courage and behave indifferently to injustice and evil in the world, it is perhaps because we do not love those who are suffering. When you are willing to suffer for them, you develop courage.

Former First Lady of US Eleanor Roosevelt said:

> You gain strength, courage and confidence by every experience in which you really stop to look fear in the face. You are able to say to yourself, 'I have lived through this horror. I can take the next thing that comes along.' You must do the thing you think you can't do.

Courage grows gradually through victories and defeat. While victories give confidence to stand up to the enemy, failures develop endurance and ability to take loss.

During the presidency of Woodrow Wilson, the United States

was having difficulties with Old Mexico. In one skirmish, American marines captured Vera Cruz. Some Americans lost their lives and their bodies were brought to New York and arrangements were made for a grand funeral.

Despite many rumours of plots to assassinate him, the president insisted on taking part in the funeral procession, His friends tried to dissuade him from going to New York saying, 'The country can't afford to lose its president.'

And President Wilson replied, 'Neither can the country afford to have a coward for president.' The president proceeded to New York and rode the procession.

Courage comes from conviction and the desire for doing the right thing. Leaders develop courage by following their conviction and enduring defeat. They take risk and plan for failures.

An Appetite for Risk

'He who is not courageous enough to take risks,' said Muhammad Ali, 'will accomplish nothing in life.' It needs courage to move forward in a path where the risk of failure is high. Every time the captain sails out, he bears the risk of running into rough weather. Yet, he sails. Leadership is synonymous with taking risk. Leaders must be ready to suffer blame before they are praised, suffer humiliation before they are honoured and suffer failures before they succeed.

Even nature has a similar story to tell. In 2004, a tsunami struck the coasts surrounding the Indian Ocean, killing over 2,30,000 people in fourteen countries, inundating coastal communities with waves up to 30 metres high, and travelling at the speed of 800 km per hour. It was one of the deadliest natural disasters in recorded history. However, before the tsunami struck the coast and the waves rose to over 30 metres, the water first *receded* to a great depth, creating the massive force leading to the tsunami.

Great leaders and entrepreneurs have been known to initially suffer much hardship, including financial losses, before they can rejoice in victory and start making profits. The gigantic corporation of today, Google, did not clear the red for many years when it started out. However, since they commercialised their search engine, they are making billions of dollars annually. Stocks that sold at the rate of $85 in 2004 became $1002 in 2013. The investors multiplied their money more than twelve times in less than nine years. The same is the story of Facebook.

Working hard to succeed and facing much to stay ahead on this path, however, does not make a leader. What makes a leader different from others is his appetite to take risks and his preparedness to suffer failures. Leaders have a long-term vision. Just like a marathon runner does not run like a sprint runner, a leader moves slowly but steadily. Even in business, people often invest in ventures which start yielding profits quickly. If you aspire to rise high, playing safe does not take you far. Industry leaders have taken many calculated risks and toiled long to reach where they are.

Suffering Accompanies Risk-taking

There is no dearth of ideas in business or politics. However, an idea has no value unless it succeeds. The only way an idea is tested in the real world is by implementation. When you are willing to take a risk, suffer losses and put at stake everything you have, people develop faith in you and your idea.

A leader takes the risk and suffers losses because he has faith in himself and his idea. That is also the only way to show to the people that he is totally committed and means business. Leaders do not seek an easy life but a life of meaning and purpose even if it is filled with pain and failures. Gurudev Rabindranath Tagore wrote this beautiful poem to express these feelings of leaders:

Let me not pray to be sheltered from dangers,
but to be fearless in facing them.
Let me not beg for the stilling of my pain, but
for the heart to conquer it.

Let me not crave in anxious fear to be saved,
but hope for the patience to win my freedom.

Grant me that I may not be a coward, feeling
Your mercy in my success alone;
but let me find the grasp of Your hand in my failure.

6

Team-building

Coming together is a beginning. Keeping together is progress. Working together is success.

—Henry Ford

No one can be called a leader if he cannot build a team. When people work in a team, their spirits get united and the whole team behaves like one man. What a formidable man that would be, since he consists of not only tremendous physical power coming from the union of people but also tremendous mental capability that comes with the union of minds. When a team is formed, it is much more than the sum total of the abilities of the members. 1 + 1 in a team is not 2 but much more. It is like the lame and blind man story. The lame cannot walk and the blind cannot see. However, when they work together, they can succeed in reaching their goal. Have you heard of this old story teaching us the power of unity?

A man once had four sons who never stopped quarrelling with one another. He was always telling them how much easier life would be if they worked together but they took absolutely no notice of him.

One day he decided to show them what he meant. He called the sons together and put a tightly tied bundle of sticks on the floor in front of them. 'Can you break that?' he asked the youngest son.

The boy put his knee on the bundle but though he pressed and pulled with his arms he could not bend the wood. The father asked each son in turn to try to break the bundle, but none of them could do it.

Then he untied the string and scattered the sticks. 'Now try,' he said. The boys broke the sticks easily in the hands.

'Do you see what I mean?' asked the father. 'If only you stand together no one can hurt you. If you all disagree the whole time and insist on going your separate ways, the first enemy you meet will be able to destroy you.'

In a good team, people complement each other rather than compete with each other. They become one, as all their strengths are complemented and all their weaknesses are subdued. That is how the magic of teamwork is created. In the words of John C Maxwell, an American author, speaker and pastor who has written more than sixty books primarily focusing on leadership, 'To collaborative team members, completing one another is more important than competing with one another.'

A leader may have millions of followers and supporters but all of them are not part of the inner core team. Team formation is the greatest job of the leader. If that is done correctly, success follows.

The Art of Team Building

We are not merely a body, which is manifested and visible to the senses, but also a soul which is invisible but is the essence of life. The body and soul are connected through different layers consisting of senses, minds and intellect as shown in Figure 1.

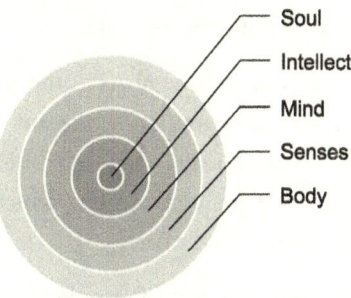

Figure 1: The representation of five realities

Thus, there are five layers of human personality. A leader's team too must have multiple layers because a leader cannot personally know more than a few men. His capacity to interact and to share the real plans and strategies is limited.

1. Core Team

Soul is the essence of being and represents the deepest level of human consciousness. When a thought penetrates to the deepest level, it becomes a belief. The core team of a leader must consist of the people who have similar beliefs as that of the leader. The core members of the team are united with the leader at the highest level. They must be free and frank with each other and enjoy equal status with the leader at the spiritual level. They must be loyal to each other, debate the issue threadbare, discuss important matters with each other and there must be absolute trust between them.

The leader, in this core team, is just the face of the team but otherwise enjoys the same status as others in the matter of sharing of thoughts. Colin Powell, an American statesman and a four-star general in the United States Army said, 'When we are debating an issue, loyalty means giving me your honest opinion, whether you think I'll like it or not. Disagreement, at this stage, stimulates me. But once a decision has been made, the debate ends. From that point on, loyalty means executing the decision as if it were your own.'

The discussion between the core members of the team is quite similar to the internal discussion that goes on inside our mind when we are trying to resolve an important issue. There are different points of view that come from different parts of the mind, which are debated and discussed and finally a decision is taken.

The members of the core team must not only be competent, but also complement each other. In order to have a winning team, you must have diverse people so that they effectively complement each other.

> Once when a lion was asleep, a little mouse began running up and down upon him. This soon awakened the lion, who placed his huge paw upon him and opened his big jaw to swallow him.
>
> 'Pardon, O king,' cried the little mouse, 'forgive me this time, I shall never forget it. Who knows but what if am I able to do you a turn one of these days?'
>
> The lion was so tickled at the idea of the mouse being able to help him that he lifted up his paw and let him go. Sometime later, the lion was caught in a trap, and the hunters who desired to carry him alive to the king, tied him to a tree while they went in search of a wagon to carry him on. Just then the little mouse happened to pass by and seeing the sad plight in which the lion was, went up to him and soon gnawed away the ropes that bound the king of the beasts.

Only a team having diverse talents can produce the result, which is far more than the sum total of the abilities of individual members. The members of the core team work closely with the leader: they rise and fall with him as they are party to all strategies employed by him.

2. Ideological Team

The second layer in the leader's team must consist of people who believe in the ideology of the leader or his 'explicit principles'. This is based on the union of intellect. These people share the same ideology which has sound principles and an overt strategy. They are the managers who are extremely good in executing tasks due to their professional abilities and training. They advise the leader and help convert his vision into reality. They help plan and frame strategies and execute the directives of the leader.

3. Propaganda Team

They propagate the thoughts of the leader in the public. They sell the idea of the leader to the people by highlighting his strengths and concealing his weaknesses. They act like salesmen of an organisation, who advertise the qualities of the leader and connect with the minds and hearts of the people. They help create the brand of the leader.

4. Followers

All leaders generally have followers, though their size and dedication may vary. Followers are like the foot soldiers of the army without whom no battle can be won. They are an integral part of the team.

Marian Anderson, an African American contralto and one of the most celebrated singers of the twentieth century, often used 'we' and 'one' instead of 'I'. When asked about this strange usage, she said, 'One realises the longer one lives, that there is no particular thing we can do alone. With the execution of the work we do, there are many people involved—those who write the music, those who make the piano on which the accompanist plays and the accompanist who actually lends support to the performance. Even the voice, the breath, the everything—it's not of our doing. So the "I" in it is very small, after all.'

Every great leader knows the importance of followers, they are the one who do the actual groundwork. They may not fully know the core ideologies of a leader, but they know what he represents. A leader must interact with his followers with great warmth as they propagate the virtues of the leader to others and garner support for him. They are like the senses of the body which help one enjoy the material things of life. A leader must, thus, keep them happy by continuously giving suitable benefits.

5. Supporters

Just like customers are important for business, supporters are important for leaders. They are not the followers as they do not work for the leaders. But their support is very crucial for the motivation and morale of the team. They vote for their leaders or buy the products and services of the company. Their numbers are the largest and their support is extremely vital. They are also like spectators in any sport, without whose presence there may not be a match. They may not play the game but get emotionally involved with the outcome of the game.

Building a Team

A team should consist of diverse people, each playing one's unique role, to achieve a common goal. Despite their diverse and even opposite personalities, they must have faith in the leader.

How is that possible?

How can positive and negative people work together?

Actually, every person has both positive and negative thoughts, for all thoughts come from the same source, which is neutral. It is your hatred against something that often creates love for another. When you have an ideology to strive for, you oppose another ideology. For example, if one is contemplating equality, he has to forego merit. Similarly, if one is thinking of promoting excellence by promoting merit, he has to fight against mediocrity and equality. Excellence and equality, though look opposite to each other, actually complement each other. Either of the extremes is dangerous. You need to strike a balance.

Hence, you must plan in advance for all opposition. Unless you have people of every shade in your team, such jobs cannot be accomplished. Each person connects with some attribute of the leader and feels at home. A team with diversity also neutralises the opposite forces and thus, balances each other.

PART VI

PRACTISING LEADERSHIP

1

Creating Trust

Trust men and they will be true to you; treat them greatly and they will show themselves great.

—Ralph Waldo Emerson

A leader may display exemplary courage, work hard and take calculated risks to get going, but unless he wins the trust of his people, he is unlikely to succeed. Brian Tracy, an American motivational speaker and author said, 'The glue that holds all relationships together, including the relationship between the leader and the led is trust, and trust is based on integrity.' Only trust can connect people, as when we trust, we expand ourselves to include others as part of us. Just like you cannot be dishonest to yourself, you also are not dishonest to one whom you really trust. Trust builds confidence in each other.

Faith means complete trust or confidence in someone or something. Faith and trust are synonymous terms, which indicate 'belief' that is not based on proof. Faith is not based on reason but emotion that comes from the heart. In many ways, faith is quite akin to love. We cannot love a person if we have no faith in that person. And when we trust a person completely, we also love him or her most deeply. A leader who is loved, is often the leader who succeeds.

> One of Napoleon's soldiers was shot at during the battle. The bullet entered near the heart.
>
> He was taken to a hospital, located in the rear where a surgeon tried to locate the bullet.
>
> As the surgeon went on with his probing, the soldier groaned, 'An inch deeper, and you will find the emperor.'

Such was the love that Napoleon commanded.

If trust is akin to love then love must also be akin to faith. Hence, we can have trust only when we have love. This is one of the oldest secrets of humanity. All religions ask their followers to love God. Bible says, 'Love the Lord with all your heart and with all your soul and with all your strength and with all your mind' (Luke 10:27).

When you have faith, no reason or evidence can change it. You find your own reason to justify faith.

> An old Christian lady used to come out of her porch every morning and shout, 'Praise the Lord.'
>
> An atheist living next door used to immediately shout back, 'There is no God.'
>
> This went on for many weeks. As time went by, the lady fell into some financial problems. So when one day she went to the porch, she asked God for groceries and then said, 'Praise the Lord.'
>
> The next day, when she went to her porch, she found all the groceries on the porch. She shouted loudly, 'Praise the Lord!'
>
> The atheist jumped from his porch and shouted, 'There is no God. I bought these groceries.'

The lady shouted again, 'Praise the Lord! He not only provided me the groceries but He also made the devil pay for it.'

The bond that exists between the leader and follower is that of faith and trust, born out of love. As long as the leaders are trusted by their followers, they shall be in a position to lead. If leaders too can develop some love for their followers, they're unlikely to break their trust.

Lincoln was a strong believer in dealing honestly with people because any dishonest action may break the trust. He once said, 'If you once forfeit the confidence of your fellow citizens, you can never regain their respect and esteem.'

The followers immediately walk out of their relationship with the leader, if their trust is broken. One single act is enough to break the trust of years. American business magnate, Warren Buffet observed, 'It takes twenty years to build a reputation and five minutes to ruin it.'

A leader has to be trustworthy to create that environment of trust between the leader and those who are led.

Steps to Be a Trustworthy Leader

1. TRUSTING YOURSELF

Who can trust a person who does not trust himself? Do you trust yourself? The answer seems to be easy and most people would say 'yes'. But that is not the reality. While others may trust you not knowing your shortcomings, you may find it difficult to ignore the truth about yourself. A trustworthy person however, has no such problem.

Golda Meir, an Israeli teacher, politician and the fourth prime minister of Israel rightly said, 'Trust yourself. Create the kind of self that you will be happy to live with all your life. Make the most of yourself by fanning the tiny, inner sparks of possibility into flames of achievement.'

In order to trust yourself, you must have integrity. There must be consistency in your thoughts, words and actions. You must say what you believe and do what you say. And your beliefs must be consistent with the belief others have in you. That is integrity. If you are doing the right thing as a matter of habit and not to create an impression or to avoid punishment, then it is integrity. While others may come to know of your failings later, you would know it immediately. Hence, before others lose trust in you, you fall in your own eyes.

Doing the right thing all the time develops a strong conscience, which deepens your conviction and further develops trustworthiness. As Einstein said, 'Whoever is careless with the truth in small matters can't be trusted with important matters.'

2. CORE BELIEF

People follow leaders through thick and thin only when they believe in what the leaders believe. If two people believe in the same God, the affinity is natural. If two people believe in the same principle, no external force is required to keep them together. They are natural allies. Thus, the relationship between a leader and his follower endures when their faiths and beliefs are same. If people with contradictory beliefs come together for a purpose, the relationship is that of mutual convenience, which breaks as soon as the purpose is served. However, when it is based on some core belief, it may last forever.

The core belief of a leader must have consistency and integrity. If the belief ever fluctuates, then no one can follow. Also, the belief of a leader must be consistent with the goals of the organisation and the universal laws.

A belief based on universal principles like justice, equality, love and compassion pertains to our consciousness or soul, so it does not change soon. Once the relationship is based on core belief, it attracts the most genuine supporters.

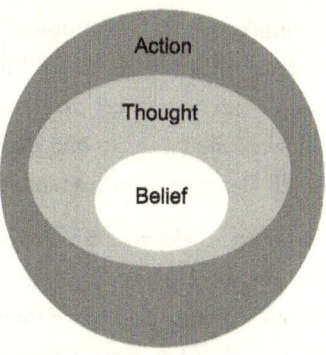

Figure 1: The representation of belief, thought and action

Figure 1 shows the relationship between thoughts, beliefs and actions. If people develop relationship with each other based on common belief, the bonding is strongest and lasts. If the relationship is based on common thoughts, it is weaker, as our thoughts and reason are not consistent. However, when the relationship is based on common action, like working in an organisation, it does not last long because such a relationship is selfish and superficial.

3. WALKING THE TALK

A true leader is one who stands by his words, whatever the cost. It is because if he says what he believes and then does not follow his word that means he has no faith in his own belief. In such a situation, how can others trust him? Hence, a leader should be very careful in committing anything or making any promise. He must properly evaluate every situation, understand the self and the opponent, and then make promises, which are realistic and achievable. He should not make outlandish promises to win the support of the followers and break them later. Once he builds a reputation, he must live by that reputation whatever be the cost.

4. TRUSTING YOUR INTUITION

It is possible to walk the talk by making your promises less challenging or by not making promises at all. Yet, that can't make you a leader.

When you make a promise, which is so outlandish that you cannot fulfil it, people lose trust in you—for not fulfilling your promise. However, if your promises are too conservative, that they do not create enthusiasm in the followers then also no one may follow you. Hence, both extremes are equally dangerous for leadership.

A leader is one who is able to make accurate predictions, and promise that which is close to reality. He makes promises which make the people enthusiastic about the future and give them hope and then he fulfils the promises as well. Leaders must have tremendous intuition and through it they should be able to visualise the future clearly. They must develop and nurture their intuition by trusting it and following its advice. Brazilian super model, Gisele Bundchen said, 'The more you trust your intuition, the more empowered you become, the stronger you become and the happier you become.'

> A small boy who was collecting money for the Springfield fire brigade went into the law offices of Lincoln. Lincoln asked him many questions about the fire brigade and seemed quite interested.
>
> 'Well, I will tell what I will do,' he said. 'I will go home to supper. Mrs Lincoln is generally good-natured after supper. And I will tell her I have been thinking of giving fifty dollars to the fire brigade. And she will say, "Abe, will you never have any sense. Twenty dollars is good enough." So tomorrow you come around and get your twenty dollars.'
>
> And the boy did get the twenty dollars.

A leader is able to anticipate the future and prepare accordingly.

5. TRUSTING GOD

'The most important lesson that I have learned is to trust God in every circumstance. A lot of times we go through different trials and following God's plan seems like it doesn't make any sense at all. God is always in control and He will never leave us,' said Allyson Felix, an American track and field sprint athlete, who won gold in the 2012 Olympics. The trust of the leader often comes from his trust in God, the Supreme Leader of the universe.

The trust in God emanates from the trust in self, because it is deep inside all of us where God resides. Those who are not connected with God may still lead people, but often they lead them to destruction, as was the case of Alexander, Napoleon, Hitler, Mao or Stalin.

Once we have faith in God, we become fearless, because by connecting with the Divine, we connect with eternity and become free from the fear of failures, infamy or death. As a famous Indian proverb goes, 'Our victory and defeat, loss and gain, fame and infamy, life and death—are in the hands of God.' One who truly believes in God fears nothing.

There is nothing impossible for a person who has faith. Jesus says in The Bible, when asked how he is able to perform the miracles which the others can't, 'Because you have so little faith. Truly I tell you, if you have faith as small as a mustard seed, you can say to this mountain— "Move from here to there" and it will move. Nothing will be impossible for you.' Yet, faith is just a word, unless it gives you courage to take initiatives that lead to the realisation of your dream.

> A man was in deep financial crisis and used to pray to God to save him by letting him win the lottery. When many days passed and the man failed to win any lottery, he said to God, 'Lord, you told us "Knock and it shall be opened to you. Seek and you shall find." Why then are you not letting me win the lottery.'
>
> Then a deep voice was heard, 'First buy the ticket.'

Mere faith is not enough if it is not followed by action. God helps only those who first help themselves.

2

Resisting Temptation

The only way to get rid of temptation is to yield to it.... I can resist everything but temptation.

—Oscar Wilde

An Urdu couplet says, 'No one gets the desired world. Sometimes we don't get the earth and sometimes we don't get the sky.' However high one may rise, however much power one may acquire, and however saintly one may turn, there is always something lacking in one's life. A leader achieves a lot in his life, but also misses out on so much more, as he is focused singularly on his goal. Though the cravings of a leader run deep, his image and persona imprison him. Bound thus, he can see everyone enjoying, but cannot venture out to lead the life of a common man.

Such is the nature of man that he takes for granted what he has, and craves instead for that which he does not have.

Leaders are often more susceptible to temptation, as in order to focus single-mindedly on one goal, they may have had to sacrifice so much that they have desired. When most of their needs remain unmet, the urge to satisfy those needs tends to get stronger as time passes. And in this condition, it may sometimes take very little to drive them to do illegal and immoral things.

You will also find many aspirants or jealous rivals who bide their time, waiting for these great leaders to fall prey to temptation. They hope to occupy the vacant positions and benefit from a leader's fall from grace.

Temptation is defined as a desire to do something, which may be wrong or unwise. This attraction is usually very powerful, and also universal like gravity. While man constantly seeks to uplift himself with great effort, it is temptation that pulls him down, turning even the most extraordinary person into an ordinary mortal.

Henry Ward Beecher, an American Congregationalist clergyman and social reformer who gained much attention for his 1875 adultery trial said, 'All men are tempted. There is no man that lives that can't be broken down, provided it is the right temptation, put in the right spot. No man is so strong that he can't be tempted.'

The great sage of ancient India and the guru of Lord Rama, Maharshi Vishwamitra too could not resist the temptation of the beautiful *apsara*–divine damsel Menaka–who enticed him even as he strived to become a *brahmarshi*–the highest sage. Bill Clinton, the former president of the United States of America presents a more recent example. He was one of the most powerful men in the world, yet got lured by an intern in the office. So many saints, politicians, scholars, businessmen and kings have fallen prey to temptation and then lost their honour, career and even life.

A seemingly powerless person can pull down a very powerful person, in no time, if he can just tempt him away from his cause. *Tao Te Ching* rightly says, 'The softest things of the world override the hardest things of the world.'

It is not that leaders do not try to resist temptation. They fully realise that they can rise higher only when they steer clear of such attractions. William Butler Yeats, an Irish poet and one of the foremost figures of twentieth century literature said, 'Every conquering of temptation represents a new fund of moral energy. Every trial endured and weathered in the right spirit makes a soul nobler and stronger than it was before.' Ralph Waldo Emerson concurred, 'We gain the strength of the temptation we resist.'

Yet, in the moments of weakness, even the greatest people fall prey to temptation.

Dissatisfaction Breeds Temptation

People tend to portray themselves as happy and satisfied, yet there is often a part of us that remains unfulfilled in our lifetime. A common man has many wishes that remain unmet. Even a saint, who resists sensual pleasures to acquire greatness, may sometimes feel frustrated. The wealthy who have much material assets have been known to crave the power that a bureaucrat enjoys by virtue of his authoritative position. Contrasted is the plight of the government officer, who represents state power, but whose income is dictated by his fixed salary. Dissatisfaction thus accosts most of us in our various roles in life. That's where temptation creeps in to wreak havoc.

Life involves many barters. We give what we have in exchange for what we do not have. Most of these exchanges are, however, termed illegal and immoral by the society. Even the wealthiest and most powerful people today do not have the special privileges that kings and emperors in the past enjoyed without violating any law, as they themselves were the law. Take the case of Alexander the great, one of the greatest leaders the world has ever seen.

> Alexander was then twenty-six years old. He had fulfilled most of his ambitions. Darius was dead, making him the undisputed

master of all western Asia. His wealth was almost boundless. His power was supreme over, what was in his view, the whole known world. But this rise took a big toll on his character. He lost the simplicity, temperance, moderation and the sense of justice that characterised his early years. Instead, Alexander adopted the Persian dress and their fondness for luxuries.

He lived in the palaces of the Persian kings, imitating all their splendour. He grew fond of convivial entertainments and wine, and often drank to excess. He acquired a *seraglio*—harem of 360 young girls, in whose company he lavished all his time. He was therefore no longer the same man. The decisiveness, the positivity and energy of character, the steady pursuit of great ends by prudence, forethought, patient effort and self-denial all disappeared. Nothing now seemed to interest him, but banquets, carousels and parties.

Get Lured by Spiritual Growth

Just like the great warrior, Alexander was lured by the physical pleasures and luxuries he had denied himself for long, Gautama Siddhartha too was enticed by another unfulfilled need. Fed up of the physical pleasures and luxuries provided by the king, who was also his father, Gautama was lured away by spiritual growth because his soul was starving. Siddhartha then gave up all the pleasures of life and set on his quest for spiritual realisation. However, few of us can be Buddhas, as most people rarely get their fill of sensual pleasures in their lives. There are more of Alexanders who aim at greatness and do much to rise high. But they constantly desire newer things, and these unfulfilled desires accumulate, ready to explode at the slightest provocation. All this temptation increases with time, seeking desperate fulfilment.

Temptation Can Corrupt

Temptation often leads to corruption and corruption can destroy the greatest leader. It is like termite eating into a mighty tree. The greatest challenge of a leader is to avoid the temptation that often accompanies success. The higher you go, the greater is the temptation. However, even a single mistake can often finish the entire career of a leader. Posterity remembers him not for the thousand good deeds, but for that one great mistake. A great leader is one who maintains his character and resists all temptation.

3

Managing in Organisations

Rank does not confer privilege or give power. It imposes responsibility.
–Peter F Drucker

Leadership is a skill that is developed gradually. In the modern world, leaders frequently occupy managerial positions instead of starting their own ventures. They have to often struggle with managing their bosses, colleagues, competitors, subordinates and customers. The management of all stakeholders is thus critical in leadership.

We can classify the different types of stakeholders that must be managed by us in such a position. The four main stakeholders are your superiors or bosses, your subordinates, your customers whom the organisation serves and your competitors who vie for the share of the pie. A schematic diagram is shown in Figure 1.

While most people are firefighting to deal with these stakeholders, a leader understands them and takes initiative to fulfil their aspirations proactively.

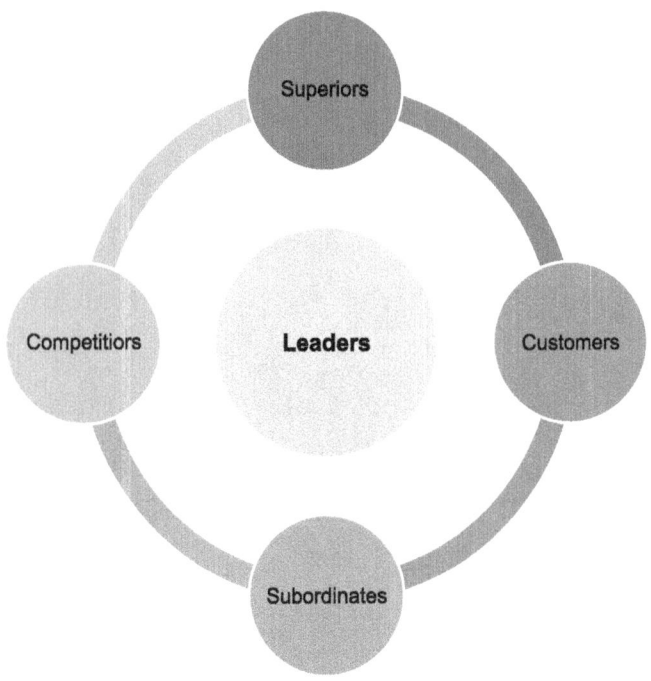

Figure 1: The stakeholders in an organisation

1. Managing the Boss

Your need to develop an understanding with the boss is paramount. He is the one who orders or controls your actions. It includes not only your immediate boss, but also all the bosses above you. Hence, understanding the boss means understanding the goals of the organisation, which is often stated in the vision and mission of the organisation.

While the followers believe in the dictum: 'Boss is always right', a leader takes initiative to understand the mind of the boss, even if it requires questioning the boss.

> Several courtiers were vying to be the royal adviser of Emperor Akbar. So one day, when they came to the court, they said to

the emperor, 'We want to be the royal advisers.' Akbar said, 'No problem, but you will have to pass the test before one of you could be my adviser.' They agreed.

The emperor unfastened his waist cloth and lay down on the floor, and asked the candidates to cover him with that cloth from head to toe. Now everybody tried to cover him, but in vain. If one wanted to cover the head, then the feet remained uncovered, or if the feet were covered, then his head remained open.

Just then Birbal entered the court, the emperor asked Birbal if he could cover him with that cloth from head to toe. Birbal paused a moment, then asked the emperor politely, 'Sir, could you pull up your knees a little bit?' The emperor did so, and Birbal could cover him from head to toe with that cloth.

Realising that they failed the test, the courtiers left the court quietly and never thought about being the emperor's adviser.

It requires imagination to think about the solution, and courage to ask the emperor to pull up the knees so that the cloth can cover his whole body. In the minds of other courtiers, either this idea had not come or they could not dare the emperor to change his posture. Birbal could do both for he knew the mind of the emperor.

You must therefore try to know what the boss wants and take necessary actions even before the boss asks you to. A leader understands the mind of the boss extremely well, even better than the boss himself, and then acts to fulfil the desire of his boss, even before he is asked.

The greatest hindrance in understanding the boss is not knowing him well. It is this ignorance that gives rise to distrust, hatred, fear, anger and suffering. Hatred may come for the boss when he is in a commanding position and controls us. It is a human weakness that we see the world from our perspective. When we look at the things merely from one perspective, we do not know the reality.

Mulla Nasruddin, carrying a chair, walked up to the owner of a second-hand store and asked how much it was worth. 'Three dollars,' said the second-hand dealer. The mulla seemed surprised. 'Isn't it worth more than that?' he said. 'Three dollars is the limit,' the owner said. 'See that? Where the leg is split? And look here, where the paint is peeling.'

'OK,' said Nasruddin. 'It was there in the front of your store with price tag of $10. It must be a mistake. I will take it for $3.'

Often, instead of understanding the boss, we expect the boss to understand us. If that does not happen, we are frustrated. We can get away with criticising any person in the world without getting adversely affected. However, when it comes to our boss, we have to suffer.

Once you tend to develop hatred against any person, you invariably misunderstand him because you interpret the signal in the opposite way like a negative of a film captures just the opposite colour. It is rightly said, 'You can't see your reflection in boiling water; truth can't be seen in a state of anger. Only a calm and quite mind sees the truth'.

When our misunderstanding grows, so does our hatred for the boss and the organisation. We are angry with the boss but we have to hold the anger as we fear the consequences of expressing it. This anger burns us from inside. As Buddha said, 'Holding on to anger is like grasping a hot coal with the intent of throwing it at someone else; you are the one who gets burned.'

If we express our anger before others, it usually gets communicated to the boss, which may further worsen the situation. Even if our criticism does not get communicated to the boss, we still remain scared.

If you analyse, there is not much that is wrong and cannot be mended. Bosses usually want efficiency, results and respect. They can give you freedom to choose your own way if you can provide what is expected of you. Their performance is also measured by your performance, so they need you to be effective. They like subordinates who can produce the results and earn them appreciation. So if you exceed your targets, so does your boss. The bosses definitely take notice of this and are prone to then give you more power and responsibility, not for your sake, but for their own sake, as you make them shine before their bosses.

You must thus identify with the goals of the boss and become an agent to fulfil his goals. You need to be on the same page as him.

The boss is as much a human being as us. We might occupy the same position as him in due course. If he behaves in a particular way, it may be due to his differing nature and greater responsibilities. He is much more accountable than us for he is not only accountable for his own actions, but also that of his subordinates. Here's an example:

> An officer was asked by his company commander to explain the error of his report.
>
> 'Sir,' the junior said. 'You know that I have four idiots working for me.'
>
> The company commander looked up from his desk and said, 'You are lucky. I have five idiots working for me.'

If you place yourself into the shoes of your boss, you can easily know his mind and develop a cordial relationship.

2. Managing Subordinates

Most people try to understand their bosses, but pay not that much attention to their subordinates. The result is that the subordinates do not perform as per expectations. As bosses, we may then develop contempt for our subordinates. We shout, ridicule and humiliate them, which results in further misunderstanding and inefficiency in the organisation. Since the efficiency of leaders depends much on the efficiency of their team, their own performance goes down if the subordinates are inefficient. This has a ripple effect in the organisation.

You cannot give a great performance, unless your team is with you on the same page. You must take initiatives to get the support of your team. First of all you must lead them by example. Be the change that you want to bring. If you want punctuality, come on time yourself. If you want their support and cooperation, give them your support and cooperation first. Respect them if you want their respect. If you expect your subordinates to know you, try to know them first. Treat everyone individually and not mechanically. Major Mach passed on this invaluable message to the graduating student-officers of the Second Training Camp at Fort Sheridan in 1917:

> You can't treat all men alike! A punishment that would be dismissed by one man with a shrug of the shoulders is mental anguish for another. A company commander who, for a given offence, has a standard punishment that applies to all is either too indolent or too stupid to study the personality of his men. In his case, justice is certainly blind.
>
> Study your men as carefully as a surgeon studies a difficult case. And when you are sure of your diagnosis, apply the remedy. And remember that you apply the remedy to effect a cure, not merely to see the victim squirm. It may be necessary to cut deep, but when you are satisfied with diagnosis, don't be diverted from your purpose by any false sympathy for the patient. Hand in hand with fairness in awarding punishment, walks fairness in giving credit.
>
> Everybody hates a human hog. When one of your men has accomplished an especially creditable piece of work, see that he gets the proper reward. Turn heaven and earth upside down to get it for him. Don't try to take it away from him and hog it for yourself. You may do this and get away with it, but you have lost the respect and loyalty of your men.

You must take the initiative to understand the needs and aspirations of your subordinates. Subordinates are your soldiers, your hands and feet, without whom you cannot perform your work efficiently.

You must never forget that as a boss, you may be the most important person in the professional life of your subordinates. Even the prime minister and president matter less to a man as does his boss. The key to make their life happy or unhappy is with the boss. We, as bosses, can make the life of subordinates hell or make it heaven. In order to become a good boss, you must understand them. Instead of getting irritated by the problems of subordinates, you must be proactive to understand and solve their genuine issues. That is the true mark of a leader.

Colin Powell said, 'The day soldiers stop bringing you their problems, is the day you have stopped leading them. They have either lost confidence that you can help them or concluded that you do not care. Either case is a failure of leadership.'

Solve the problems of your subordinates and you will win their loyalty. They work for you with their full commitment and you grow as a leader.

3. Managing Customers

Every organisation is there to serve people whom we call customers. A government provides administration to people, police organisations reduce crime, revenue department collects revenue for the country, a manufacturer produces quality goods and a service provider gives service to the customer.

We all know what is expected from an organisation. It is often stated in its vision and mission statements. However, when we become part of an organisation, we often do not see our organisation from the perspective of our customers. Instead of listening to them, we find them as irritants who are always complaining and never seem to be satisfied.

Bill Gates once said, 'Your most unhappy customers are your greatest source of learning.' It is because behind every complaining customer, there are hundreds of unsatisfied customers who may not complain, but then they may choose to go with your competitors, at the earliest opportunity. They may never come back to you again. The very survival of the organisation depends on the customers. If the customers go to your competitor, your organisation is ruined and soon you may well be out of your job. It may be worthwhile to remember the words of US business magnate Henry Ford, 'It is not the employer who pays the wages. Employers only handle the money. It is the customer who pays the wages.'

Customers are the real employers of people in the business world. Take care of them through proper initiative and you win their loyalties forever.

4. Managing Competitors

Life is like a game, which everyone wishes to win. A leader faces competition from within the organisation and also from without. The first competition of the leadership is from within. Everyone within the organisation wishes to expand their area of influence and power. Hence, you are often squeezed from all sides. The bosses want to impose their will and see that the things are done their way while the subordinates want their own way.

There is also external competition from competitors. You must keep a close watch on them and know not only the initiatives taken by them but also the possible initiatives to become more competitive. Instead of following them, you must outsmart them by being one step ahead in taking initiative.

You have to take care of all your competition by taking the right initiatives. Like chess, you must make your move after duly understanding your competitors. You must play a proactive role in this.

You must understand your customers and satisfy them in the best possible way. You must try to stay a couple of notches higher than your competitors. There is no place for complacency in this competitive world. Once you lose the race, you may never be able to come back again.

Creating Excellence

While most people merely firefight to solve problems which are most urgent, a leader must deal with not only the immediate problems but also prevent future issues. Albert Einstein rightly said, 'Intellectuals solve problems, geniuses prevent them.' Leaders ensure that the problems are identified in advance and solved even before they really become a problem. Author Arnold Glasow said, 'One of the tests of leadership is the ability to recognise a problem before it becomes an emergency.' Once the problems are reduced, leaders can devote more time for future planning and fulfilling the vision of the organisation. They can take proactive measures to eliminate the problems from arising and create excellence within the organisation.

4

Decision-making

Nothing is more difficult, and therefore more precious, than to be able to decide.

—Napoleon Bonaparte

'Sir, what is the secret of your success?' a reporter asked a bank president.

'Two words.'

'And, sir, what are they?'

'Good decisions.'

'And how do you make good decisions?'

'One word.'

'And sir, what is that?'

'Experience.'

'And how do you get experience?'

'Two words.'

'And, sir, what are they?'

'Bad decisions.'

The greatest ability of the leader is his ability to take the 'right' decisions. There are many methods that help take these decisions. One way is to follow the popular opinion and decide the issue on the basis of consensus or majority opinion. This approach is quite easy and also popular as it takes care of public will. When people are happy, the leader becomes popular; he is a 'people's man'. Yet, taking a 'popular decision' does not always mean you are taking the 'right decision'. There is a Chinese proverb, 'A wise man makes his own decisions, an ignorant man follows public opinion.'

One who decides on the basis of popular opinion is actually not a leader, but a follower as he follows public opinion. He does not need any vision for such decision-making. They are quite popular in the short term, but often turn unpopular as time progresses.

Effective leaders however, think about the long-term consequence of their decisions rather than their immediate popularity or condemnation. Like a good surgeon, they operate the wound and try to cure their patient rather than allowing him to live with a painful wound. Like a doctor, good leaders do not take populist decisions. They do not provide sweet medicines to the patients simply because they would like it. It is often the bitter pill which cures.

Peter F Drucker, the legendary management guru, explains the inevitability of taking hard decisions in his book, *The Effective Executive*, 'And it is at this (final) point that most decisions are lost. It becomes suddenly quite obvious that the decision is not going to be pleasant, is not going to be popular, is not going to be easy. It becomes clear that a decision requires courage as much as it requires judgment. There is no inherent reason why medicines should taste horrible but effective ones usually do. Similarly, there is no inherent reason why decisions should be distasteful but most effective ones are.'

Good leaders take effective decisions even if these decisions are criticised by everyone, and they have the courage to stand by them.

> United States Senator, Benjamin Wade of Ohio, Henry Winter Davis of Maryland and Wendell Phillips were strongly opposed to President Lincoln's re-election, and Wade and Davis issued a manifesto. Phillips made several warm speeches against Lincoln and his policy. When President Lincoln was asked if he had read the manifesto or any of Phillips' speeches, the president replied:
>
> 'I have not seen them, nor do I care to see them. I have seen enough to satisfy me that I am a failure, not only in the opinion of the people in rebellion, but of many distinguished politicians of my own party. But time will show whether I am right or they are right, and I am content to abide its decision.'
>
> 'As to those who, like Wade and the rest, see fit to depreciate my policy and complain at my official acts, I shall not complain of them. I accord them the utmost freedom of speech and liberty of the press, but shall not change the policy I have adopted in the full belief that I am right.'

Leaders do not avoid decision-making, and those who do cannot be leaders.

What are the right decisions?

A right decision is one which can achieve the desired result. The test of a decision is not its popularity, but its power to achieve the goal. Just like a shooter's efficiency is measured by how close his arrow is to the bull's eye, the efficiency of the leader is judged by his accuracy in achieving the goal.

Making the right decision is important for good leadership as people gradually start believing the words of leaders who repeatedly achieve what they promise.

Even good decisions can fail, unless the leader does constant follow-up during its execution stage. A leader should try to convince people before a decision is taken so that more people develop ownership of the decision and attempt to make it a success. The resistance to the decision needs to be minimised, and the support for the decisions should be multiplied for its success.

Most people like to go with a decision, which is likely to succeed. However, when they fear failure, they dissociate themselves with the decision lest they are accused of supporting the wrong decision. Hence, the reputation of the leader in taking correct decisions plays an important role in the success of a decision.

If the leader is known to be a good decision-maker, more people would support the decision due to their faith in the leader and that would invariably improve the chances of success.

The success of a decision is based on good strategy, which is unique in each case and is often unpredictable. A good decision-maker calculates many moves in advance—not only his own, but also of the opponents and develops an exhaustive plan to overcome the challenges that may come in the way of its implementation. All the strategies remain stored in the mind of the leader, and it is revealed only on a 'need-to-know' basis.

Leaders have to be fully responsible for the outcome of their decision, even if it was based on the suggestions of many people.

Steps in Decision-making

The best decisions are made by a combination of a rational mind and an intuitive heart. Leaders are known to use intuition even if there is a large amount of ready data available for decision-making.

We can, however, improve our choices by following some standard procedures.

1. Understanding a Problem

The first step to solve a problem is to understand the problem. Just like even the best medicines are of no help if the diagnosis is wrong, even the best decision is bound to fail if the problem is not fully comprehended.

> Two salesmen were sent to an African country by a shoe manufacturing company to scout new markets where they could sell their company shoes. The salesmen spent a couple of weeks there, then came back to report their findings to their manager.
>
> The first salesman said, 'There is no market in that country. I did not see anyone wearing shoes there.'
>
> The second salesman said, 'There is a huge market for shoes in that country. I did not see anyone wearing shoes there.'

You can easily decide which conclusion is correct. We must ask the right questions to know the right answers. The problem must be analysed properly, and the source of the problem must be identified. What factors are responsible for the persistence of the problem? How can these problems be eliminated?

The problems must be first classified into the following categories:

1. **Urgent Problems:** There are many problems which are unique and unpredictable needing urgent solution. You can't predict eventualities like fire and so when there is a fire, we must first resort to firefighting, and then try to analyse the problem and try to prevent it in future. Urgent problems need innovative solutions and are best solved by intuition and experience. A leader however, does not leave

the problem after it has been taken care of but goes deep into the root of the problem and then finds a solution which can prevent such problems from occurring in future.
2. **Routine Problems:** There are many problems which crop up in our lifetime due to the inherent nature of our being. For example, if we are not careful about the hygiene of our food, drinks and environment, we are likely to fall sick. These problems can be removed by cleaning the surrounding to remove their cause. In organisations too, certain types of problems are encountered regularly, which are due to some inherent weakness of the organisation. We then need systemic changes to eliminate them forever.
3. **Systemic Problems:** Many issues in organisations run much deeper and need long-term efforts for cure. These require painful decisions, which can be termed surgical. The process has to be slow but continuous to weed them out.

2. Finding Solutions

There can be a number of solutions to the same problem, as there are multiple medicines out there to cure the same disease. If the same patient goes to a number of doctors for advice, they are all likely to prescribe different medicines. Further, one must also understand the natural ability of the body to overcome any disease. Hence, sometimes even taking rest and allowing the body to take care of the disease could be a good method to cure a disease. So every problem need not to be given top priority nor should be immediately taken up for remedy. Einstein said, 'Not everything that counts can be counted, and not everything that can be counted counts.'

Why should you waste your energy on something that does not matter much or which is probably just a temporary problem like the fatigue of the body, which anyway disappears once a person gets good sleep? It is often better to let people solve their own problems, without the leader interfering. This helps the organisation too, as more people develop problem-solving ability.

Leaders discuss their problems with their colleagues to list out as many alternatives as possible. They discuss the pros and cons of each alternative, honestly and sincerely. As every alternative is likely to invite an opposite view, hence, a calculated risk has to be taken. It is only in simple problems that we can have clear-cut solutions. A complicated and old problem has no simple solutions. Instead, you require a multi-pronged approach, where you may have a plan A and plan B and even plan C for backup.

A leader has to finally decide which solution has the greatest chance of success. Once the solution is adopted then the whole team must support the decision.

3. Effective Implementation

A great idea means nothing, unless it is implemented. The success of an idea depends on the execution of the idea. Leaders are not men of ideas but those who are known for implementation of the ideas. When an idea is implemented, people see the benefit of the idea and develop faith in their leaders.

A leader must build a team of leaders who are guided by the same vision and mission as that of the leader and put the idea into practice.

5

Cultivating Leaders

Leaders don't create more followers, they create more leaders.

—Tom Peters

The previous chapter revealed how leaders can implement their vision only when they have a strong team. Let us take it further.

Just like when iron remains in the close proximity of magnet, it becomes a magnet, those who stay near leaders gradually become leaders. The job of a good leader is to create more leaders because it is much easier to lead the leaders than the followers. You have to only guide these leaders, no hand-holding is required. However, in the case of followers, you have to personally lead them all the way.

Just like a seed becomes a tree laden with fruit, because the tree is already hidden in the seed, though not visible, leadership too is hidden in people. You only have to nurture it. In the words of the Scottish novelist John Buchan, 'The task of leadership is not to put greatness into people, but to elicit it, for the greatness is there already.'

The cultivation of leaders is not very different from the cultivation of crops by a farmer. It follows the same rules.

1. Picking up the right seeds
2. Removing the weeds
3. Creating suitable ground
4. Producing leaders

1. Picking Up the Right Seeds

Vince Lombardi, the American football player, coach and executive, who is considered to be one of the best and most successful coaches in National Football League's history said, 'Leaders aren't born, they are made. And they are made just like anything else, through hard work. And that's the price we'll have to pay to achieve that goal, or any goal.'

Anyone can be a leader if he has a burning desire to be one. Unless people have ambition, drive to work hard and vision, they can't be made leaders. Leaders identify among their followers the potential leaders and then groom them to become be leaders.

Just like a farmer picks up the best seeds for sowing, a leader selects the best followers for nurturing them to leaders.

2. Removing the Weeds

Every farmer knows how dangerous the weeds are and how they can arrest the growth of any crop. If the weeds are not removed regularly from the ground, they would not let the crop grow.

In the same way, the weeds of mediocrity, lethargy, lust and greed are present in everyone and in every society, which prevents the growth of leadership in an organisation. It is the job of the leader to remove such elements from the organisation and also from the individual minds. This can be done by discouraging, punishing and even removing people who are incompetent, inefficient and corrupt from the organisation.

When you do nothing against such people, it is difficult to create leaders in any organisation.

3. Creating Suitable Ground

A good follower learns more from the action of the leader than from his words. Yet, in order to allow the leadership to grow to its highest potential, it is important to create proper ground for the leadership to flourish in the hearts and minds of the followers.

William James, an American philosopher and psychologist who was also trained as a physician, wisely said, 'The deepest principle in human nature is the craving to be appreciated.' Everyone craves for appreciation as it nourishes the soul. Developing the habit of appreciating the followers for every single good job and helping them to correct their faults is one of the greatest methods of creating leaders.

> Louis XIV had a delicate manner of paying compliments. When he nominated De Lamoignon as president of the parliament, De Lamoignon went to thank the king.
>
> 'There is nothing to be thankful for,' said the king, 'because if I had found a better and braver man I would have nominated him instead of you.'

Condemnation on the other hand kills the soul. It may be the right weapon to be used against the enemy and 'weeds' but must not be used with friends, followers and potential leaders.

Leaders must also be fair and just to create the right ground for leadership. They must judge people by results, and not by methods. There are numerous methods to do the same job and a creative person not only finds new methods to do the same job, but soon is able to find the most efficient method to achieve the performance. Hence, even creativity is tested when people are allowed to follow their own methods while doing the job. Take the case of General Grant whose work was appreciated by President Lincoln even though his actions were not in agreement with the views of the president. Lincoln wrote a letter to Grant on 13 July 1863, which read as follows:

> I do not remember that you and I ever met personally. I write this now as a grateful acknowledgment for the almost inestimable service you have done the country.
>
> I write to say a word further. When you first reached the vicinity of Vicksburg, I thought you should do what you finally did— march the troops across the neck, run the batteries with the transports, and thus go below, and I never had any faith, except a general hope, that you knew better than I, that the Yazoo Pass expedition and the like could succeed.
>
> When you got below and took Port Gibson, Grand Gulf and vicinity, I thought you should go down the river and join General Banks, and when you turned northward, east of Big Black, I feared it was a mistake.
>
> I now wish to make the personal acknowledgment that you were right and I was wrong.

General George Patton, a United States Army general, best known for his command of the Seventh United States Army and later the Third United States Army in the European Theatre of WWII, said aptly, 'Never tell people how to do things. Tell them what to do and they will surprise you with their ingenuity.'

Leaders must ensure that followers are awarded for their merit and their hard work is well-appreciated and recognised. Once people know that their performance alone matters, everyone would give their best and the leaders can easily select the leaders for different types of assignments. When proper ground is created, leadership flowers naturally. Jesus Christ explained the mystery in the following parable:

> A farmer went out to sow his seed. As he was scattering the seed, some fell along the path, and the birds came and ate it up. Some fell on rocky places, where it did not have much soil. They sprang up quickly, because the soil was shallow. But when the sun came up, the plants were scorched, and they withered because they had no root. Other seeds fell among thorns, which grew up and choked the plants. Still other seeds fell on good soil, where it produced a crop—a hundred, sixty or thirty times what was sown. Whoever has ears, let them hear. (Matthew 13:3-9)

A leader creates such a ground in his organisation that thousands of leaders bloom to carry on his vision and mission.

4. Producing Leaders

With constant effort and supervision, gradually leaders are able to produce a large number of leaders who are not only like them but even better than them.

These leaders are not the replica of their leaders, but have the DNA of their leaders, just like children have the DNA of their parents. They carry forward the legacy of leaders. They are the new generation leaders having more enthusiasm, better capability and better vision of the coming world. They can better connect with the new generation and lead them to a glorious future.

6

Leaving a Legacy

A good name is more desirable than great riches; to be esteemed is better than silver or gold.

—Proverbs 22:1 (Bible)

There are billions in this world, but few leaders. Yet, these few leaders represent the billions. The history of the world is nothing but a tale of great leaders. Every person is a follower of one or the other leaders of present or past. Every person who is born has to die, yet every person continues to live in this world, not only in the flesh and blood of his children, but also in the minds of those who follow his thoughts. Whatever we do, our future generation has to pay.

A signboard outside a restaurant read:

'Eat as much as you can and let your grandchildren pay the bill.'

A man entered the restaurant, ate as much as he could, and when the waiter gave the bill he pointed to the signboard, 'Don't you see, only my grandchild needs to pay for this bill.'

The waiter said, 'Sir, this is not your bill. This is your grandfather's bill.'

We are paying for what our ancestors had done, and we are also reaping the fruits of their labour. Good leaders always try to leave the world better than what they inherited. The good actions and thoughts of our past good leaders still motivate us today, while the thoughts of bad leaders continue to misguide people even today.

In 1962, events in South East Asia meant that large-scale army recruitments were being undertaken. Despite not meeting the physical requirements, eighteen-year-old Anna was selected, as emergency recruitment was taking place. While in the army, he contemplated suicide owing to the tough life and the constant state of deprivation of his family and village. He even wrote a suicide note, but decided against this, as his sister's wedding had to be fixed. A vehicle in which he was travelling was hit by a bomb, but he survived. This led him to dwell on the purpose and meaning of life and death.

In a book stall, at the New Delhi station, he came across a small booklet by Swami Vivekananda, titled, *Call to the youth for nation building*. He realised that saints sacrificed their own happiness for that of others, and that he needed to work towards ameliorating the suffering of the poor. He led the greatest anti-corruption fight in India, and today, he is one of the most respected leaders of India.

His name is Anna Hazare

Swami Vivekananda was one of the greatest spiritual leaders of India of the nineteenth century, who died in 1902. Yet, more than six decades later, his one book changed the thought process of a man who was almost on the verge of suicide, to start a new life and build a new India.

Legacy of a Leader

A leader becomes great when he leads large number of people to a common goal based on a common ideology. Gandhi is not the name of a person, but a symbol of an ideology, which is popularly known as Gandhism, which encompasses truth, non-violence, non-cooperation with evil. Hitler today is not the name of a person made of flesh and blood, but symbolises an ideology, popularly called Nazism, which is based on his thoughts and actions.

Every great leader represents a philosophy and when he leaves the world, people carry on his legacy whether it is good or bad. The imprint of an individual's action is carried by his children, who are closely influenced by the person. But the imprint of a great leader is there on millions of people. When Jesus was hanged on the cross, he had only twelve disciples, who too were killed soon. Yet, his legacy continues, and today, even 2000 years after his death, there are billions of people who are influenced by his thought and carry forward his legacy. JR Miller, a popular Christian author and the pastor of several churches in Pennsylvania and Illinois, wrote:

> Yet, there are things—virtues, fruits of character, graces, victories of moral conquests, which men do carry with them out of this world. Someone says, 'The only thing that walks back from the tomb with the mourners and refuses to be buried is character.' This is true. What a man IS, survives him. It never can be buried. It stays about his home when his footsteps are no longer heard there. It lives in the community where he was known. And that same thing—what a man IS—he carries with him into the eternal world. Money and rank and pleasures and earthly gains—he leaves behind him, but his character, he takes with him into eternity.

We do not wish to be known as evil, even after we die. It is because we all live in this world in many ways. The children whom we love and the people who repose their trust in us continue to be identified with us. They are respected for our good deeds while they are condemned if we are bad.

The world is quite interconnected and every person is related to others in many ways. When a father does something wrong, his children suffer and when children commit mistakes, the parents are blamed. When one politician is arrested for corruption, the credibility of all politicians takes a beating.

In the same way, when one individual of a country wins a Nobel Prize, the entire country celebrates. When that one football team, consisting of few individual footballers wins a game, the whole nation is filled with joy. We are all related to each other, and are influenced by the good and bad behaviour of our leaders. While individuals affect a few people, good leaders affect millions. Hence, they must be more responsible as they are not fighting the battle for the self, but for the millions of people. They are not struggling to brighten the present; they are striving to build the future.

> Marshal Lyautey was visiting a forest that had been devastated by fire.
>
> He said, 'We must replant cedars.'
>
> His friend said, 'You can't mean that. They take two thousand years to grow to their full height!'
>
> 'Two thousand years?' said the surprised Lyautey. 'In that case, my friend, there is not a minute to lose. You must get on with it right away.'

Great leaders leave great legacies that influence future generations. They may continue to influence the world forever, as they live in the hearts and minds of people, where they achieve immortality.

Bibliography

1. 'Anna Hazare', *Wikipedia*, http://en.wikipedia.org/wiki/Anna_Hazare
2. 'A Nice Catch', http://english.specialist.hu/a3/xfun/jok.php
3. 'Avaricious and Envious', *Aesop's Fable* http://renaissancewave.blogspot.in/2009_02_01_archive.html
4. 'Bharti Airtel becomes the fourth largest mobile operator in the world', http://www.airtel.in/about-bharti/media-centre/bharti-airtel-news/corporate/bharti-airtel-becomes-the-fourth-largest-mobile-operator-in-the-world]
5. 'Brand Power To The People: J&J Takes Lead In Forbes Ranking', http://www.forbes.com/sites/jenniferrooney/2011/10/05/brand-power-to-the-people-jj-takes-lead-in-forbes-ranking/?partner=yahootix]
6. 'Broken windows theory', *Wikipedia*, http://en.wikipedia.org/wiki/Broken_windows_theory
7. 'Chanakya', University of California, Computer Science Alumni, Riverside http://alumni.cs.ucr.edu/~nkumar/story.html
8. 'Charisma', *Wikipedia*, http://en.wikipedia.org/wiki/Charisma
9. 'Dhirubhai Ambani Biography', http://www.iloveindia.com/indian-heroes/dhirubhai-ambani.html
10. 'Doctor's Meeting', *Joke Buddha* http://www.jokebuddha.com/Confessed#ixzz2jpMyQ5h6
11. 'Ekla Chalo Re', *Wikipedia*, http://en.wikipedia.org/wiki/Ekla_Chalo_Re
12. 'Eleanor Roosevelt Quotes', https://www.goodreads.com/author/quotes/44566.Eleanor_Roosevelt
13. 'Electrostatic induction', *Wikipedia*, http://en.wikipedia.org/wiki/Electrostatic_induction
14. 'Fear is the Key', http://alumni.cs.ucr.edu/~nkumar/story.html

15. 'Four Sons - if you stand together no one can hurt you', *Aesop's Fables*, http://www.frtommylane.com/stories/helping_others/four_sons.htm
16. Greek Legend: Alexander and the Pirate, 'Mythology and Folklore Readings: Content for a course in Myth & Folklore.' University of Oklahoma. http://mythfolklore.blogspot.in/2013/07/greek-legend-alexander-pirates.html
17. 'Jack Welch', *Wikipedia*, http://en.wikipedia.org/wiki/Jack_Welch
18. 'Leadership'—a speech by Maj CA Bach, Leadership and Initiative—Law of Success—Napoleon Hill—Master Mind Books, India
19. 'Lesson in Lateral Thinking: The Tale Of Two Pebbles', http://www.debonoconsulting.com/Lateral-Thinking-Lesson-Pebbles.asp
20. 'Mullah Nasruddin Jokes', *Hazarbuz Website* http://hazarboz.tripod.com/id19.html
21. 'Parable of the snake': http://vmbhonde.wordpress.com/2011/06/17/snake-and-saint/
22. 'Some 437,000 people murdered worldwide in 2012', UN crime agency reports http://www.un.org/apps/news/story.asp?NewsID=47544#.U0u_qlWSxMA
23. 'Stories of Birbal - Akbar's Advisor', http://www.bharatadesam.com/literature/stories_of_birbal/stories_of_birbal_10.php
24. 'Sunil Mittal Profile', http://www.iloveindia.com/indian-heroes/sunil-mittal.html
25. 'Sufism/Nasrudin', *Wikibooks*, http://en.wikibooks.org/wiki/Sufism/Nasrudin
26. 'The Ass and the Lapdog', *Aesop's Fables* http://www.worldoftales.com/fables/Aesop_fables/Aesop_Fables_3.html
27. 'The Bat, the Birds, and the Beasts', *Aesop's Fables*. The Harvard Classics http://www.bartleby.com/17/1/24.html
28. 'The Fox and the Cat', *Aesop's Fables* http://www.worldoftales.com/fables/Aesop_fables/Aesop_Fables_8.html
29. 'The Lion and the Mouse', *Aesop's Fables*. http://www.umass.edu/aesop/content.php?n=21&i=1
30. 'Think different', *Wikipedia*, http://en.wikipedia.org/wiki/Think_different
31. 'This Was Bapu', URL: http://www.mkgandhi.org/students/thiswasbapu/foreword.htm
32. 'We shall fight on the beaches', *Wikipedia*, http://en.wikipedia.org/wiki/We_shall_fight_on_the_beaches
33. Abbott, Jacob. *Alexander the Great* http://www.mainlesson.com/display.php?author=abbott&book=alexander&story=deterioration&PHPSESSID=374147b005af3ecbddff3e4b9266d2f8
34. Badenhausen, Kurt. 'Tech Rules List Of The Best Brands' *Forbes*. http://www.forbes.com/powerful-brands

35. Bejorna, Lena. 'To Conquer The Island You Must Burn The Boats.' http://whoislena.com/to-conquer-the-island-you-must-burn-the-boats/
36. Frank, TA. 'A Brief History of Walmart.' First published in the April, 2006 issue of *Washington Monthly* http://reclaimdemocracy.org/brief-history-of-walmart/
37. Miller, JR. 'The Making of Character' http://gracegems.org/Miller/the_making_of_character.htm
38. Reagan, Ronald. *On the Eve of My Meeting with Gorbachev*, The Heritage Foundation http://www.heritage.org/research/lecture/on-the-eve-of-my-meeting-with-gorbachev
39. Schreck, Julius. *The Leader's Travels* URL: http://thecensureofdemocracy.150m.com/life3.htm
40. Sudarsono, Danny. 'Why was Vietnam a mistake?' http://blogs.swa-jkt.com/swa/10350/2012/01/11/why-america-failed-the-vietnam-war-one-of-the-factors/
41. Broket, LP. *The Life and Times of Abraham Lincoln*, Jones Brothers & Co. Publishers, 1865
42. Blumenthal, Karan. *Steve Jobs: The Man Who Thought Different-A biography*, Bloomsbury Publishing, 2012
43. Carnegie, Dale. *How to Win Friends and Influence People*, Vermilion, 2006
44. Cathecart, Thomas & Klein, Denial. *Plato and a Platypus Walk into a Bar: Understanding Philosphy through Jokes*. Penguin Books, 2008
45. Dehlvi, Sadia. *Sufism, The Heart of Islam*, HarperCollins Publication India, 2010
46. Dobelli, Rolf. *The Art of Thinking Clearly*, Sceptre, 2013
47. Drucker, Peter F. *The Effective Executive*, HarperCollins, 2009
48. Joshi, Manik. *Best Jokes: I Have Ever Heard - 888 Jokes*, Kindle Edition, Amazon Digital Services, 2014
49. Kushner, Malcolm. *The Humor of Ronald Reagan: Quips, Jokes and Anecdotes from the Great Communicator*, Kindle Edition, Museum of Humour.com Press, 2012
50. Lala, RM. *Touch Of Greatness: An Encounter with the Eminent*, Penguin Books, 2002
51. Machiavelli, Niccolo. *The Prince*, Penguin, 2011
52. Maurus, J. *Anecdotes of the Great: That Help to Build a Better Life*, Better Yourself Books, 2012
53. Mcclure, Alexander K. *Lincoln's Yarns and Stories*, The John C Winston Company, 2014
54. Müller, F Max. *Ramakrishna: His Life and Sayings*, CreateSpace Independent, 2007
55. Mital, GS & Gupta, Manju. *1221 World's Choicest Jokes*, Jaico Publishing House, India, 2011
56. Rollins, Alfred B Jr. *Roosevelt and Howe*, Transaction Publishers, 2001
57. Welch, Jack. *Winning*, HarperCollins Publishers, 2005
58. Wordsworth, RD. *"Abe" Lincoln's Anecdotes and Stories: A Collection of the Best Stories Told by Lincoln, Which Made Him Famous as America's Best Storyteller*, Nabu Press, 2010